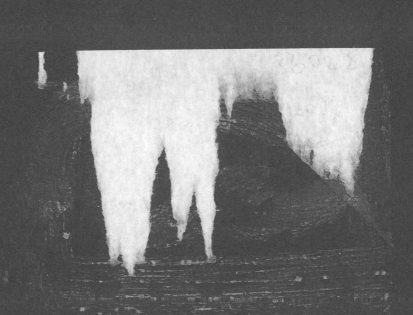

THE
BOOT

For Larah

Published in 2010 by Laurence King Publishing Ltd
361–373 City Road
London EC1V 1LR
United Kingdom
Tel: + 44 20 7841 6900
Fax: + 44 20 7841 6910
e-mail: enquiries@laurenceking.com
www.laurenceking.com

A catalogue record for this book is available from the
British Library.

ISBN: 978-1-85669-663-0

Design: Studio8 Design
Illustrations: Lovisa Burfitt – www.agentsandartists.com
Picture Editor: Heather Vickers

Printed in China

THE BOOT

BRADLEY QUINN

LAURENCE KING PUBLISHING

INTRODUCTION

Well-heeled women have always worn boots. Shoes may be able to carry a woman around town, but showing off a pair of boots can be reason enough to leave the house. Women love boots because they are walking signifiers of extravagance and imagination, and because they communicate something about the body that shoes don't. Boots can create an aura of masculinity and authority yet be feminine and seductive at the same time. And women everywhere are powerfully aware of this fact.

Boots are about style, not fashion. They have always represented something radical for women, because for most of their history boots were considered to be male attire. They resurfaced in fashion as an antidote to the frou-frou femininity of Dior's postwar New Look, and with them came an element of sex appeal. Decades earlier, Coco Chanel had discovered the way in which elements of masculine attire could be sexually provocative when worn by women, and she realized that a woman wearing men's footwear was embracing something forbidden. A woman in boots was an outsider at best; she was individual, unpredictable, daring and transgressive, and had a style of her own. The boots on her feet were not simply expressions of fashion, but an expression of the woman herself.

With boots come mystery, excitement and allure, yet also protection and practicality. Boots have walked the world for centuries on the feet of nomads, soldiers, travellers and horsemen, fortifying them against the elements while enabling them to stand their ground. Many of the styles that today we consider to be modern were first worn by men in earlier centuries and have since been redesigned in a feminine guise. Contemporary boots incorporate all the variations seen in other fashion footwear, from shapely heels, precipitous stilettos, vertiginous platform soles and pointed toes, to zipper closures, shiny buckles and serpentine laces. Women's boots came into fashion in the 1960s, and were highly popular by the end of the following decade. Their appeal has grown steadily since then, to the extent that they have become a staple of almost every woman's wardrobe. In the first years of the twenty-first century, the styles and variations of boots launched each season is staggering – the fact that they are now as popular as shoes and sandals shows what a great leap forward they have made in a relatively short period of time.

Opposite:
The lace-up boots of the Victorian and Edwardian eras made their mark on modern fashion. The mid-calf rise, pointed toes and sculpted wooden heels that characterized them set the standard for many popular boot styles to come.

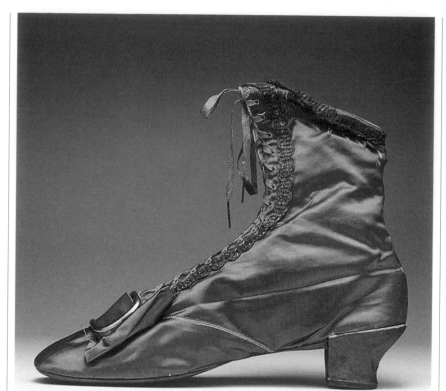

This book is intended to mark this high point in the boot's long evolution. Chapter one – 'The History of the Boot' – charts how boots changed from rudimentary hides bound to the feet in ancient times, to icons of the futuristic Space Age style that gripped Paris in the 1960s, to an essential element of any woman's wardrobe in the twenty-first century. Boots became the only fashion item that were as appropriate for the boardroom as they were for a countryside hack on horseback, and the second chapter, 'Urban Chic', chronicles the designers and styles that by the 1980s had made them a staple of city dressing.

The link between sex and shoes has never been disputed, and boots take sex appeal to a higher level. The third chapter, 'Seductive Soles', describes why men love women in boots, and why women feel sexier and more powerful with a pair of boots on. Chapter four, 'Style Tribes', takes a journey around the world to discover exotic styles, uncovering the rich patterns, vibrant colours and lavish motifs of the cultures of Asia, Africa and the Americas and their hold on fashion designers. Chapter five, 'Slick Surfaces', explores the meanings that are assigned to surfaces, investigating a variety of bootmaking materials and their histories. The chapter reveals that fur, rubber, snakeskin and exotic leathers are loaded with symbolism, proving that the outermost layer of the boot is more than just skin deep.

Although rarely discussed in fashion, the impact of the street on boot design has been considerable. Chapter six, 'Street Style', explains why this has created significant differences between shoe and boot styles. Designer shoes are typically born as secondary lines in high couture, and trickle down to street footwear, while high-end boot styles often exist on the street before surfacing on couture catwalks. Whether worn on the street, in battle, or elsewhere, tough women have always loved boots. Chapter seven, 'Warrior Women', explores why images of women in battle and of superheroes fascinate boot designers, and showcases a range of styles that make women look and feel empowered.

Right now boot design is regarded as one of the richest areas of innovation in fashion. The final chapter, 'Future Strides', charts the exchanges between material science, cutting-edge technology and boot design. New techniques, smart substances, intelligent interfaces and sensory surfaces hold the potential to radically redefine boots, yet the touch of the human hand still remains. Boots are the ultimate mélange of traditional craftsmanship, new technology and luxury materials. As today's designers update the styles of the past with fresh visions of tomorrow, they move forward into an exciting future that will change boots forever.

1
HISTORY

ANCIENT BOOTS

Long before they marched into the fashion limelight, boots exerted a powerful influence over events throughout the world. From their first appearance on the feet of early men and women, boots made it possible for whole nations to migrate across the ice caps and for legions of warriors to hold fast in battle. Worn by early humans long before the sandal existed, primitive boots may even have produced lasting physical changes in the human foot, uncurling our ancestors' primate-like toes and aligning them with the rest of the foot. In so doing, boots anchored early humans to the ground and enabled them to take up a stance.

Evidence of boots and shoes dates back to the Palaeolithic period: traces of a moccasin-like footprint have been found in France, left in a cave roughly 40,000 years ago. Skeletal remains at a late Palaeolithic site in Russia were found with remnants of animal hides and ivory beads spread across the foot, ankle and shin, indicating that boot-like footwear dates back at least 29,500 years. These primitive boots were fashioned from pieces of animal hide, which were crudely bound to the leg, and probably stayed on the wearer's feet for most of his or her life.

As civilizations evolved so did footwear, and the presence of boots in early wardrobes says much about the cultures that wore them. The recent find of a pair of boots dating to around 3300 BC reveals that the early humans of central Europe lagged behind their Eastern neighbours in terms of what they wore on their feet. Discovered on an Alpine man frozen and mummified in a glacier in Italy, the boots were constructed with bearskin soles and deerskin uppers, and stuffed with dried grass to insulate the feet and cushion the soles. Straps crafted from lengths of woven grass laced them crudely to the wearer's feet, which probably made them uncomfortable to wear and somewhat unwieldy to move in.

Yet while Ötzi the Iceman, as he has been dubbed, and his people were foraging for berries and herding sheep in their primitive boots, cultures in many other parts of the world had long been wearing more sophisticated footwear. Mummified remains of tartan-wearing Europeans dating back to 4000 BC have been discovered in China; these are believed to have been nomadic cousins of the Celts. One of the women was buried in a long red dress with deerskin boots. Superbly crafted in soft leather, her boots were knee-high and sculpted closely to her calves for comfort and ease of movement. Worn today, they would be considered the height of fashion.

Evidence of the wearing of boots is also found in the ancient civilizations of central Asia from the fourth millennium onwards. Stone tablets depict the Assyrians wearing robust boots as they hunted wild animals and waged war against their neighbours; yet scenes of ceremonies and court life rarely include boots, indicating that they were never considered part of a formal wardrobe. By contrast, stone carvings made by the Hittites show processions of men wearing leather ankle boots crafted with elegantly upturned toes: not only were boots a part of court life, but they were made in styles that reflected the fashions of the day.

Ancient carvings made by the Sumerians show soldiers in knee-high boots suitable for riding horses; and boots were essential wear for those who steered chariots, as they deflected any gravel or small stones thrown up by the galloping horses. Boots seem to have evolved slowly until the time of the Scythians, a nomadic society that emerged during the eighth century BC, and bred horses, tanned hides and dyed leather. They lived in the vast steppelands of Central Asia, stretching eastwards from the Black Sea. Remains of high leather boots that fit tightly to the ankle and calf have been recovered from Scythian burial sites, suggesting that they created the first riding boot, a legacy that has lasted for 3000 years.

Recent archaeological evidence from burial sites has suggested that the Scythians might have been related to the famous mythical women warriors known as the Amazons, whose beauty, ferocity and bravery were described by the Greek historian Herodotus, but who until recently have been considered merely the stuff of legend – albeit very powerful legend. But it seems that real-life female warriors existed among the Scythians and the Sarmathians, a neighbouring people, and such women rode horses, hunted and fought in battle. As depicted in art and described in literature, the legendary Amazons appropriated male boots and weapons for their own use. Dresses were simple and cut short for riding horses, while close-fitting trousers were tucked into high boots. Armed with bows, spears, axes and shields, and wearing helmets

Opposite:
Some of the earliest depictions of female boots date back to the time of the Hittites, with boots crafted from untanned leather fastened to the leg, and laces made from vegetable fibres or lengths of animal hide.

and men's boots, they are distinguishable from men in ancient artworks by the fact that they often wear a single earring.

Boots were popular with the ancient Greeks, who sometimes even embellished them to reflect fashion trends. As draping techniques were developed to create low-cut, ankle-length dresses for women, cobblers began to distinguish between the right foot and the left, and introduced a variety of fashionable and practical boot styles for both soldiers and civilians. High boots were worn by warriors: Mycenaean soldiers, for example, wore sandal-like vamps attached to armour-like leather gaiters that protected the lower leg, while warriors from Orchomenus wore leather ankle boots dyed crimson to distinguish them clearly from their enemies.

Civilian men and women wore styles such as the 'embades', a low boot crafted in a soft leather that covered the entire foot and the ankle, and which was often lined with felt or fur. Their name comes from the verb meaning 'to step into', as the wearer would have had to slide his or her foot into the boot. Embades worn by women were often embroidered, or were even decorated with gold lace.

The Greeks took bootwear to new heights around the fifth century BC, when they introduced the lofty 'kothornos', a boot with a thick platform sole. These boots were invented by the tragedian Aeschylus, who introduced them in theatre. He scaled the height of the actor's sole according to his character's importance, so that gods and heroes appeared to be far taller than mere mortals. The sole of the kothornos was constructed from leather or cork and attached to a soft leather upper that extended to mid-calf or even as far as the knee, and laced up the leg with leather straps. Audiences left the theatre convinced that shoe height should be equated with status, creating a brief vogue for thick soles. Although the trend was short-lived among the Greeks, it would be returned to with zeal nearly two millennia later, when the high-soled 'chopine' was considered the height of ladies' fashion in Venice, and Louis XIV of France popularized the elevated 'Louis' heel for men.

In ancient Rome, urban ladies are believed to have worn raucous footwear that was criticized for making too much noise. Historians claim that footfalls made by wooden-soled clogs could be heard at a considerable distance, and leather ankle boots were said to have squeaked with every step. Gladiatrices, as female gladiators were called, wore armour, helmets and footwear that made them virtually invincible. Their boots were similar to those worn by male gladiators, crafted from leather parts and metal studs, and typically laced thigh-high.

Boots took a leap forward under the Byzantines, whose emperors wore purple boots similar to those of the Greeks, embroidered in gold with double-headed eagles. However, as the Byzantines embraced early Christian concepts of clothing, they brought about radical departures from Classical styles. According to Christian practices it was inappropriate to expose the body, so by the eighth century, shoes and boots, designed to cover the feet, replaced sandals. Goatskin ankle boots with pointed toes were popular among Coptics and other Christian groups, generally worn under sweeping robes. The pointed-toe styles they wore harkened back to the Sumerians, yet also sparked a trend that became popular in Europe for hundreds of years, and even set a standard for medieval footwear.

Above:
The well-made boots of classical antiquity were heavily embellished and crafted from leather dyed to reflect the wearer's rank. Fashionable men and women wore boots made from the finest leather, providing comfort as well as durability.

Opposite:
Sixth-century Roman women wore many styles of boot, depending on their social standing and the activity they were carrying out. Robust boots such as these were most likely worn for outdoor activities.

NATIVE AMERICANS

Huge differences in both climate and terrain across the vast American continents gave rise to different ways of life and styles of clothing among the indigenous cultures. In the Subarctic and Arctic regions of the north – including Alaska, northern Canada, and Greenland – boots were worn by both men and women all year round. Boots in these regions advanced to be water-proof, to provide traction on ice and snow and to insulate the feet in one of the coldest climates on earth. With no written history, it is hard to determine exactly when such footwear originated, but by the sixth century AD knee-high boots had evolved from moccasins, made from tanned hides sewn with tiny stitches. The tanning technology is thought to have been based on that used by the Scythians a thousand years earlier. Aided no doubt by their prowess on horseback, the Scythians' techniques spread northwards throughout Asia, and from there across the Bering Strait.

Subarctic and Arctic peoples adapted their boots to conditions. Light-weight summer boots were made from sinews taken from the caribou's back region, while winter boots were cut out of the caribou's hide, which was turned outwards to yield a stronger grip on snow and ice. In the Arctic, the northern Inuit and the Yupik wore the soft boots known as the mukluk or kamak, which were made of reindeer hide or sealskin. The boots weighed little and allowed hunters to move quietly and to feel the ground beneath them with their feet.

In more southerly regions of North America, Native Americans often went barefoot. However, when they did wear footwear, they usually wore some form of moccasin – a word coming from the Algonquian language to denote footwear that ranged from slipper-like mules to high-topped boots. Some type of moccasin was used by almost all of the more than three hundred Native American tribes. From Saskatchewan to Sonora, most forms of boot were originally made of soft leather stitched together with sinew. Tribes living on rocky terrain used hardened rawhide for the sole, while others used fur to line the leather to give added warmth. Most crafted the boot as a single, waterproof unit, but those worn by Plains women were made from legging-like thigh-high leathers sewn to the moccasins to create a one-piece shape.

Native American footwear has a long history of embellishment, and the shapes embroidered on boots range from large-scale representations of animals to intricate patterns. Algonquian peoples, for instance, wore winter boots made from moose hide and embroidered with porcupine quills and strips of fur. Trade with Europeans introduced the Native American people to colour-ful glass beads. Boots were often adorned with pom-poms and feathers, and decorated with bands of embroidered fabric or leather panels cut into fringes. Although Western footwear is seldom so highly decorated, Native American styles inspired a number of Western styles, including modern slippers, loafers and boat-shoes.

The pre-Columbian peoples of Central and South America also wore boots, albeit not usually as lavishly embellished as those made by the North American tribes. The Incas, whose empire emerged from the highlands of Peru in the early thirteenth century and flourished until the sixteenth century, combined a sole made from fibres harvested from the agave cactus with uppers made from animal hide. Men's boots were usually high enough to cover the knee, while women's rose to the ankle. The boots worn by royal Incan women were the flashiest by far, made from gilded leather, signifying the high status of the wearer and her worth to the tribe.

In Mexico, the militaristic Aztecs flourished from the fourteenth to the sixteenth century. Aztec warriors wore the cozehuatl in battle, a boot with a sandal-like sole joined to armour-like legging that protected the shin and knee. Shielding the lower legs was a priority for Aztec soldiers, who disabled enemies in battle by crippling their legs and feet. The Aztecs avoiding killing their enemies, preferring to take them alive so that they could sacrifice them to their gods after the battle was over.

In Patagonia, the Spanish colonizers discovered very large tracks left by the native people and believed that they belonged to a race of giants, which they named 'Patagones', meaning 'with big feet'. In fact, the size of the footprints was due to the fact that these 'Patagones' wore guanaco (a type of llama) hides wrapped around their feet and legs, padded generously with grass, to protect them from the cold.

Opposite:
Moccasins such as these from the 1890s are still made and worn by Canada's Native peoples. The basic boot style is similar all across the region but each people employs characteristic distinguishing embellishments.

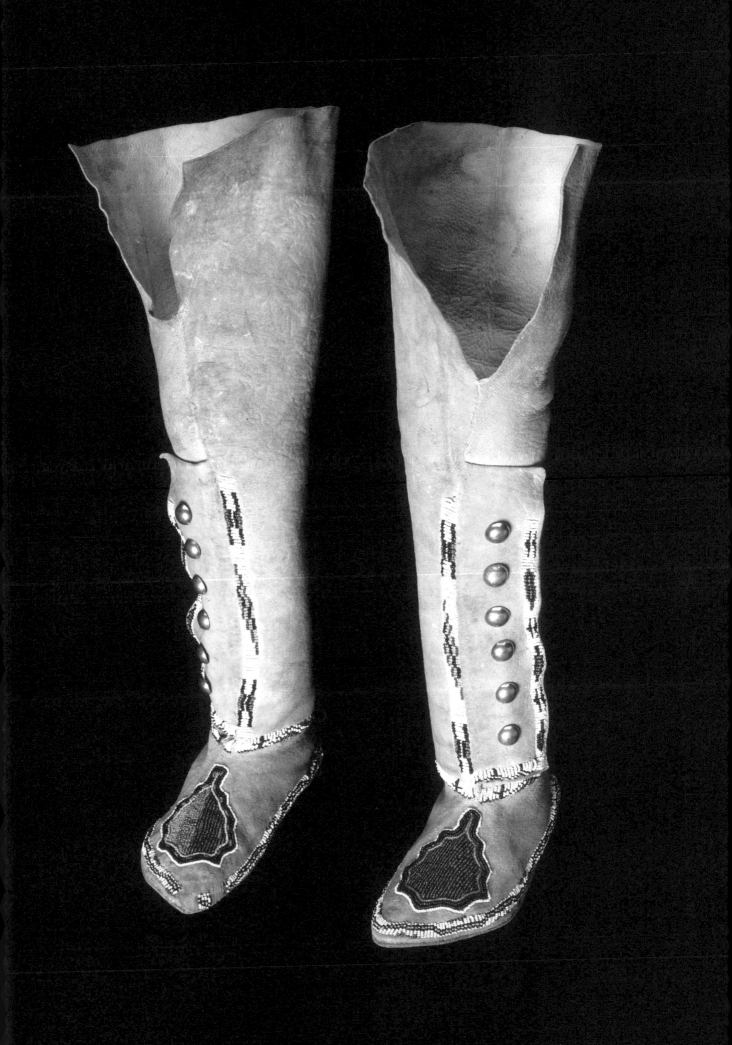

EARLY EUROPEANS

Medieval boots were originally a two-piece unit consisting of a simple shoe and a robust legging that extended up to the knee or even the hip. They were widely flared at the top – so much so that French cobblers called them 'bote', a term the English adopted around 1066 after the Normans crossed the Channel, and subsequently anglicized as 'boot'.

For several centuries, the French had worn low boots in styles deriving from the Vikings, whose customs, hairstyles and clothing exerted a great influence over Northern Europe from around the ninth to the eleventh century. Boots with pointed toes were a Viking favourite, but they also wore boots with rounded toes. The Vikings made boots well, reinforcing them at the heel and toe, and often fitting straps, laces or toggles over the instep. Metal buckles to fasten boots and gaiters had been used in France since Merovingian times (c.500–750 AD).

When the 'bote'-wearing Normans appeared in England, they must have seen the shapeless, low-rise footwear worn by the Anglo-Saxons as old-fashioned, perhaps even shoddy – men and women wore tunics of varying lengths, and the well-off wore simple ankle-high boots over thick woollen hose held up by garters. Their footwear was made by the 'turnshoe' technique of sewing the sole and the upper together inside out and turning them right-side out when finished. Shoes made in this way were crafted without left or right orientation and could be worn on either foot. For those rich enough to afford them, the high-topped French styles would have provided considerably more protection and warmth for the legs, both in battle and in civilian life.

Above:
Medieval boots were simple in style, but complicated to walk in. The sole was merely a piece of smooth leather that provided little traction, and the tapering toes protruded from under the long tunics worn at the time.

Opposite:
By the fifteenth century, the style of boot worn was an indicator of status, power and style, making embellishment an important feature. Both men and women wore stylish boots accessorized with buckles, bows and jewels.

Boots disappeared from women's wardrobes for much of the Middle Ages, as it became fashionable to wear shoes or slippers indoors and to step into a protective outer sole when venturing into the street. A style known as a 'chopine' was introduced in Venice around 1400: this was a vertiginous platform-soled mule, held in place by leather straps, which raised the wearer off the ground, sometimes by as much as 60 centimetres (two feet). The chopine served both a practical and a symbolic purpose. Its thick sole lifted the wearer's feet and hemline well above the often filthy streets, while the height it added symbolically implied the high social standing of the wearer.

Towards the end of the fifteenth century, Polish-made 'Poulaines' became popular in France, then spread across Europe. The Poulaine was a shoe with extremely long, impractical toes. The points were stuffed with moss or reinforced with whalebones to hold their shape. Poulaines were worn with 'patterns' (sandal-like clogs) when the wearer ventured into the street; the sole of the patterns was wood, the upper was fabric or leather. The front and back ends of the soles were tapered so wearers could move forward by rocking slightly.

At the end of the fifteenth century, pointed toes were replaced by wide-toe styles, known variously as the 'cowmouth', the 'bearpaw' and the 'hornbill'. In Elizabethan England, footwear for men and women had rounded toes made with a low, flat, one-piece sole. Greek comedies were popular at the time, and some of the footwear worn on stage contributed to vernacular fashion. A soft, heel-less fabric boot worn in Greek comedy, the 'soccus', was referred to as a 'sock'. A high-soled boot similar to the Greek kothornos was referred to in the theatre as a 'buskin', from which the term 'busker' was derived, describing an itinerant actor who performed for donations on the street. This is not to be confused with another buskin, which was a generic name for boots rising higher than the ankle but lower than the knee: these had been in currency in England since 1503, perhaps inspired by an earlier French style known as 'brousequin' or perhaps from the Dutch style known as 'brosekin'.

As Europeans became wealthier, the upper classes began to distance themselves from the masses through conspicuous refinement and extravagant ornamentation. Boots were seen as somewhat unsophisticated, and they were eschewed in favour of high-heeled footwear not associated with riding or warfare. Footwear made of expensive silks expressed the leisurely lifestyles and accumulated wealth of the 'well-heeled'.

In the seventeenth century, celebrated French shoemaker Nicholas Lestage may have unknowingly imitated a technique used by North American Indians, when, in 1663, he made seamless calfskin boots for Louis XIV. By peeling the hide from the calf's leg rather than cutting it away, he created a unique design crafted without seams in the side. Lestage was forbidden by the king to make boots for others or reveal his technique, which was kept secret for more than a century after his death.

Throughout the eighteenth century, a variety of boot styles was worn by men, but women wore mainly delicate court shoes, mules and shapely high heels. Riding boots were an exception, but for women they were cut much lower than men's boots. The word 'buskin' was revived to describe high-heeled, laced ankle boots worn by men at this time, which inspired a trend in female footwear a century later.

Eighteenth-century footwear was made on straight lasts, without a sole designed specifically for the left or right foot. Boots and shoes were uncomfortable and people frequently switched footwear from one foot to another to soothe their pain. Comfort improved as ladies' shoes were crafted with wooden pegged soles and rolled shank undersoles that provided better arch support, but up until the mid-nineteenth century most shoes continued to be made on absolutely straight lasts, with few cobblers differentiating between feet.

From about 1830, women's skirts became ever wider and more of the leg was exposed when walking, making the female foot and ankle visible. The immense wire-framed crinolines introduced in the 1850s were wider and significantly lighter than padded undergarments had been, with the result that a gust of wind, an awkward step, or a slip sideways could reveal the wearer's legs. Fashion dictated that women's feet should appear small and delicate, so they were typically compressed in tight-fitting boots – like the corset that bound the torso and made the waist seem smaller, the ankle boot functioned as a device for making the feet appear to be narrow and petite.

Women's lace-up boots first became popular in England during the 1830s, when the consort of King William IV, Queen Adelaide, made them fashionable. Known as Adelaides, the boots were side-lacing and waterproof, allowing women more freedom of movement outdoors. With the invention of vulcanized rubber around 1840, it became possible to make boots with elastic

panels on the sides, making them more comfortable to wear and easier to pull on and off. This style was revived in the 1960s for men and women, and variously named the Chelsea boot and the Beatle boot.

By the 1860s, the Adelaide had evolved into a boot that rose to mid-calf, and became popular when Queen Victoria wore it at Balmoral Castle. Known as a Balmoral, the style featured a plain, tapered square toe and a vamp much like a riding boot. It was designed to be comfortable for wear outdoors, but also to keep ankles tightly laced out of view (Queen Victoria believed that bare ankles were likely to arouse men, so should be concealed as far as possible).

Ankle boots became higher, rising towards the knee and sporting a higher heel, in both North America and Europe. As pointed toes and rounded toes went out of fashion, boots with square toes became popular and remained in vogue for the next 50 years. Few working-class women in Britain wore boots until the end of the century, when the advent of the sewing machine made it possible to mass-produce boots at an affordable price. Along with mass production came metal eyelets and rubber heels, which respectively made boots quicker to lace and more comfortable to wear.

The 1880s saw stylish Parisian women stepping out in beautifully embroidered boots with 'Pinet' heels, which were a tapered version of the Louis heel previously in vogue. Boots designed by Jean-Louis François Pinet were among the most beautiful ever made, and are regarded today as masterpieces of workmanship and decoration. The materials he chose were the most resplendent ever seen in footwear, and included brocade, painted leather and embroidered silk. Pinet's influence extended beyond Europe and his work had a huge impact on American footwear. As mass production improved, American versions of Pinet's styles became widely popular.

At the end of the nineteenth century, sports were popular among women, and rubber-soled boots were a popular choice for tennis, croquet and cycling. Bicycle boots had low heels, pointed toes and high laces, and like other high-top boots used for sport, were worn with shorter skirts. Outdoor sports gave women leisure activities that had previously belonged almost exclusively within the masculine sphere, allowing men and women more common ground.

Above left:
Victorian women believed that boots were more decorous than shoes, as they covered the feet and lower legs. Many women wore boots several sizes too small to make their feet appear smaller and more dainty.

Above right:
When it came to sport, women's footwear had traditionally been limited to riding boots, but in the nineteenth century, rubber-soled boots were introduced for such sports as cycling, badminton, and apparently even baseball.

Opposite:
Boots designed by legendary bootmaker Jean-Louis François Pinet created a legacy of style. Their shapes, silhouettes and materials attest to the supreme skill with which they were designed and crafted.

MODERN WOMEN

By the era of the First World War the role of women was starting to change, and clothing began to reflect this. Shorter hemlines made shoes more popular and the boot began to disappear from fashion: it was seen as restrictive and uncomfortable, while lightweight shoes matched the new freedom that women felt. As more of the ankle and leg came into view the modern fashion silhouette began to form, with the shoe as the cornerstone of the new look. High heels visually slimmed the foot and ankle as boots had done, and tightened the calf muscle to add shape and definition to the lower leg. During the war years themselves, lace-up boots came back into fashion, valued for their practicality and durability.

The styles of the 1920s made the foot a focal point in fashion to an extent that had never previously occurred. Practical boots were replaced by shoe styles that reflected the new trend for streamlined, simplified clothing. Shoes with low heels, closed toes and leather soles were the most popular, held in place by crossover bars or T-straps that fastened around the ankle.

A number of fashion's most legendary footwear designers emerged in the 1930s, with visionaries such as Salvatore Ferragamo and André Perugia exploring new materials and forging fresh styles. A shortage of leather and a wartime ban on rubber inspired them to experiment with new materials, and the platform soles they crafted from wood, cork and other elements would prove influential for decades. Perugia introduced elastic, sock-like boots with platform soles in the 1930s, a style that women would wear again in the Space Age craze of the 1960s.

For most of the 1940s, footwear took a back seat, and boots virtually disappeared from fashion altogether. Dior's New Look at the end of the decade heralded a return to classic femininity with a corseted waist and wide skirt. The style was worn with heels from such designers as Charles Jourdan – who would set a standard for elegant boots two decades later, which were created by streamlining earlier styles. Designers such as Roger Vivier challenged conventional shapes and construction techniques. Vivier cut away toes, reconfigured the vamps and moulded the heels into new shapes, creating a trademark style that he later adapted for boots.

Many boots made during the 1950s were mass-produced and therefore affordable, but they were rarely regarded as fashionable. Women from all walks of life could afford good shoes and chic footwear was less of an indication

Opposite:
Knee boots were an essential part of the 1960s wardrobe, worn by women of all ages and from all walks of life. As hemlines rose, so boots became higher, and on London's King's Road they were the height of fashion throughout the decade.

Right:
Crammed into the upholstered boot of a convertible, British-born Hollywood actress Olivia de Havilland flaunts her riding boots as she exchanges horse power for four-wheeled transport.

of status than ever before. Shoes did not begin to creep past the ankle again until the end of the decade, when the cinematic world seemed to be filled with boots. Western films introduced cowboy boots into mainstream menswear, while science fiction brought ankle boots into vogue for both men and women. The elastic-sided Chelsea boot was first produced in the late 1950s, and was out-selling most other boot styles by the end of the 1960s.

The Flower Power youth of the 1960s set out to change the world; the freedom and self-expression they fought for was embodied in fashion and foot-wear alike. The boot styles of science fiction came to life in Space Age fashion, as Paco Rabanne, Pierre Cardin and André Courrèges created a fresh, overtly futuristic look. New technology made innovations in footwear possible, and synthetic materials, metals and plastics replaced traditional leather and cloth. Such colours as white, silver and electric blue evoked the palette of the future. As designers experimented with colour combinations, textures and shapes, the demand they created for boots was huge. Boots became an emblem of youth culture, representing freedom, optimism and self-expression.

An eighteenth-century men's boot made a comeback in 1961 when it was radically redesigned as the 'pant boot' and worn underneath women's trousers. Mary Quant's injection-moulded ankle boot of 1964 heralded a fresh generation of bootwear, and British boutique Biba sold some the edgiest styles imaginable. In the hands of Beth Levine, Roger Vivier and Salvatore Ferragamo, materials such as 'mock croc', two-tone suede and stretch fabric came to characterize the era. Maud Frizon, a former fashion model, is known for the zipless boot that she designed in 1969. Mary Quant, the creator of the miniskirt, launched a full footwear range, Quant Afoot, in 1967, with fluorescent yellow ankle boots that were a cutting-edge take on the traditional 'welly' boot.

As the decade continued, boots crept higher up the calf, past the knee, and didn't stop until they reached the top of the thigh. Go-go boots, first designed by Courrèges and given a boost in popularity by Nancy Sinatra's song 'These Boots Are Made For Walkin', became a symbol of 1960s cool. Courrèges later launched a knee-high version of the boot, which was considered the height of Space Age chic. When Yves Saint Laurent sent Roger Vivier's thigh-high boots down the catwalk with a miniskirt he was offering a radically alternative vision to that of the New Look that Dior had launched two decades earlier.

The boots designed in the 1970s are among the most expressive ever made. Like the 1960s styles that preceded them, they were shiny, colourful, textured and patterned, but by the end of the decade boots were also studded,

Above:
Boots were often symbolic of the resistance that characterized the counter-culture and social revolution that emerged during the 1960s. As young women began to rebel against the conservative norms of the time, their dissent was often reflected in their choice of footwear.

Opposite, top left:
In 1964, French designers presented the Space Age look, with white boots, aerodynamic hats, box-shaped dresses and dress suits with skirts that soared above the knee.

Opposite, top right:
When fashion designer Mary Quant introduced the miniskirt in 1964, fashion was changed forever. The mini was worn by every young fashionista in the Western world – as were high boots.

Opposite, bottom:
Boots were an important part of the 1960s fashion silhouette, complementing the streamlined shapes and minimalistic styles popular at the time.

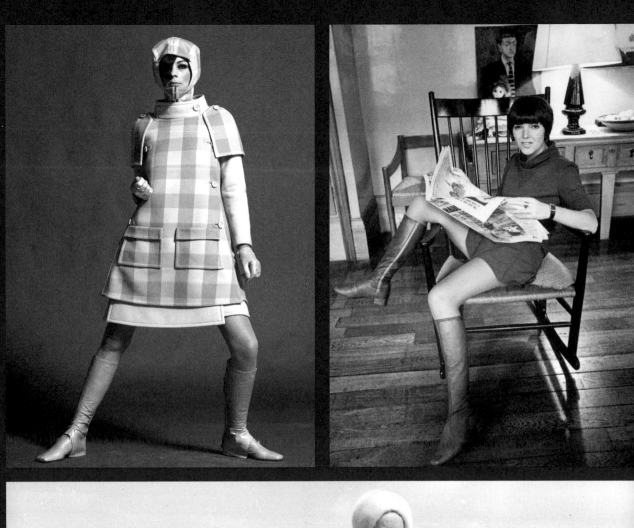

bejewelled and covered in psychedelic appliqués. Leather virtually disappeared from bootwear, as did conventional soles. Wedge heels and platform soles – a favourite of disco dancers – dominated the high street as well as the dance floor, where they were sometimes combined with stacked heels that could measure up to 20 centimetres (eight inches) high.

When it came to footwear, the well-heeled found more inspiration on the feet of celebrities than they did on the fashion catwalks. Glam bootwear worn by Elton John and Cher marched off the stage and straight into shoe shops. Film and television, equally, had a profound influence on what people wanted to wear on their feet. Movies such as *Saturday Night Fever* depicted boots that were fabulous and fun, while female characters on TV shows such as *Charlie's Angels* and *The Bionic Woman* fought with booted karate kicks and crushed villains underneath platform soles. Superheroes such as Wonder Woman created a vogue for spectacular boots, which women would wear with hot pants or short skirts. Boot styles worn in subcultures including punk, glam and heavy metal came on to the catwalk, influencing fashion and achieving cult status. Vivienne Westwood was one of the first designers to link footwear directly to subcultural styles, launching her fetish boots in 1976 as part of the infamous 'Bondage' collection. Elements of country and western culture came into vogue at the same time. As stars such as Dolly Parton gained fame, cowboy boots emerged as fashion wear around the middle of the decade.

The fashion of the 1980s is often remembered for its excesses – power-dressing, flash jewellery, shoulder pads and designer labels. Fashion trends were also inspired by sports clothing: sporty trainers dominated urban streets while legwarmers wrapped bare legs in soft textures. Trousers and legwarmers were typically tucked into boots, although some fashionistas wore them stretched over boots. In 1980 the film *Urban Cowboy* catapulted cowboy boots into mainstream fashion, and leather returned as the bootmaker's material of choice. Footwear designers were quick to introduce other mid-calf styles such as the ruched slouch boot and the pirate boot, which was crafted in supple leather with tops that could be folded down to reveal a contrasting lining. Shoe designer Claudia Ciuti introduced a new boot style with double-stitched central seams running up the front of the upper, joined to an elevated crepe sole that got higher at the heel. The music scene continued to play a part in footwear trends, with the New Romantics of the very early 1980s popularizing historical styles, while lace-up Dr. Martens became mainstream wear.

Opposite:
These boots, from Spanish designer Loewe's Autumn/Winter 2007 collection, recall the style of the swashbuckling boots worn at the court of Louis XIV, as shown on page 20.

Right:
British designer Vivienne Westwood has long found inspiration in historical themes, which she reinterprets with an often outrageous twist in her clothing, accessories and footwear designs.

As the decade drew to a close, the inherent elegance of classic boot styles was rediscovered. A trend for elegant, well-tailored 'dress boots' made bootwear a staple of women's winter wardrobes. Designers such as Stéphane Kélian, who combined his trademark Parisian elegance with comfort and chic, designed braid-trimmed boots that brought a classy accent to any fashion item. Italian fashion designer Sergio Rossi considered boots and shoes to be an extension of a woman's body rather than an accessory, and many of the boots he designed during the 1980s continue to look contemporary today.

By the 1990s, it was clear that boots were no longer confined to a handful of casual styles and worn only in winter. Available in any conceivable style and made for any occasion, boots had a permanent place in every woman's wardrobe. And with the boot regarded as a fashion staple rather than an optional accessory, footwear designers began to view this as an area of where experimentation and innovation could thrive.

Historically, women's fashion boots had been based on male footwear and divested of their functional origins. During the 1990s, riding boots and military styles were revived and slightly streamlined to suit an urban wearer, and the waterproof 'wellies' worn in the countryside became a city mainstay during wet weather. Reference to other classic styles abounded as the decade continued. Patrick Cox designed elegant fur-lined boots inspired by the Belle Epoque, while Bruno Magli launched low-heeled patent-leather designs that paid homage to Courrèges.

Although footwear designers had long associated shoes with sex, mainstream boots had not been viewed through erotic eyes until now. Boots had traditionally been worn to conceal the foot and leg, but new styles introduced in the 1990s became curiously provocative. Designers cut away the toe to bring lacquered pedicures into view and removed whole panels to reveal racy tattoos and fishnet tights. Designers such as Versace and Thierry Mugler showed fashion collections inspired by fetish wear, which included the 'kinky' boots more associated with S&M subcultures than high fashion. Biker boots, another subcultural style, came to the Paris catwalks when Chanel's designers decorated them with the label's signature logo and showed them with elegant evening dresses.

Conversely, dressy boots, recognized for their potential to dress up almost any ensemble, also gained ground as fashion classics. High-heeled boots became a favourite of urban women everywhere, who were just as likely to wear them into a board meeting as they were to pull them on with a pair of jeans. Flat boots remained both elegant and practical, the wearer being able to tramp through rain or snow and still arrive with attractive footwear, not to mention dry feet.

Although the boot has remained a fixed point in human dress for several thousand years, it is one of the least-changed of all fashion items. Despite their long history, boots have been slow to benefit from the same ergonomic studies conducted on conventional shoes or the technology invested in high-performance footwear. Yet as the demand for boots continues to grow, shoe technology is being developed especially for boots, and composite materials promise to create new levels of comfort and bold new aesthetics. Twenty-first-century boots seem poised to take a dramatic step forward; just as they helped to shape the ancient world, they seem destined to shape the future.

Above:
Italian footwear designer Sergio Rossi introduced boots that were effortlessly modern. His trademark elegance is reflected in boots that are form-fitting and feminine.

Opposite:
The Autumn/Winter 1998 collection was one of John Galliano's first for Christian Dior, injecting contemporary fashion with sixteenth-century splendour. The thigh-high boots Galliano presented echoed the styles worn by King Francis I of France.

JOSEPH AZAGURY

British designer Joseph Azagury established his label in 1990, and since then his footwear has gained recognition as one of the country's most elegant brands. His shoes and boots are decidedly modern yet resonate with influences from the past.

Azagury studied at the Cordwainers College in London, where he became acquainted with historical styles and with traditional techniques, and his knowledge of these areas clearly informs his work today. Traditional hobnail boots and classic

Balmorals, for example, are given new life as striking, elegant designs that perfectly accessorize present-day fashion. Whereas historically such styles were usually hidden underneath long skirts and flowing gowns, today they are on full view, and Azagury's attention to detail transforms them into eye-catching boots that could even risk upstaging the rest of a wearer's ensemble. Button-up seams and high-lacing uppers merge traditional and modern design in a single boot.

Although Azagury's designs may bear traditional details and offer a nod to history, the level of comfort and support they provide the wearer is nothing but modern. Stretch materials are used in some models to enhance their comfort and extend their durability, at the same time making them easier to pull on and kick off. Some of Azagury's most arresting designs are boots that look like shoe–boot hybrids: his platform boot appears to wedge the foot between a high heel and a peep-toe wingtip; his square-toe

crocodile boot features an Oxford lace-up section across the upper.

Azagury's designs have always had a strong fashion signature; his business was originally run from the exclusive boutique of his brother Jacques, one of the UK's top couturiers. Like his brother's fashion collections, Azagury's footwear expresses couture sensibilities, highlighted by the exquisite craftsmanship and individual flair with which his boots and shoes are created.

ABOVE: Often finding inspiration in period styles, Azagury has imbued these high-button boots with the elegance of the late Victorian era.

OPPOSITE: Although the design is completely contemporary, the profile of these high-cut, high-heeled lace-up boots recalls the styles of the early 1900s. Azagury's boots are cut close to the body to emphasize the shape of the foot and calf.

OVERLEAF: The starting point for Azagury's boots is often a sketch such as these. The drawings enable him to perfect the boots' proportions, profiles and details before he begins crafting them in leather.

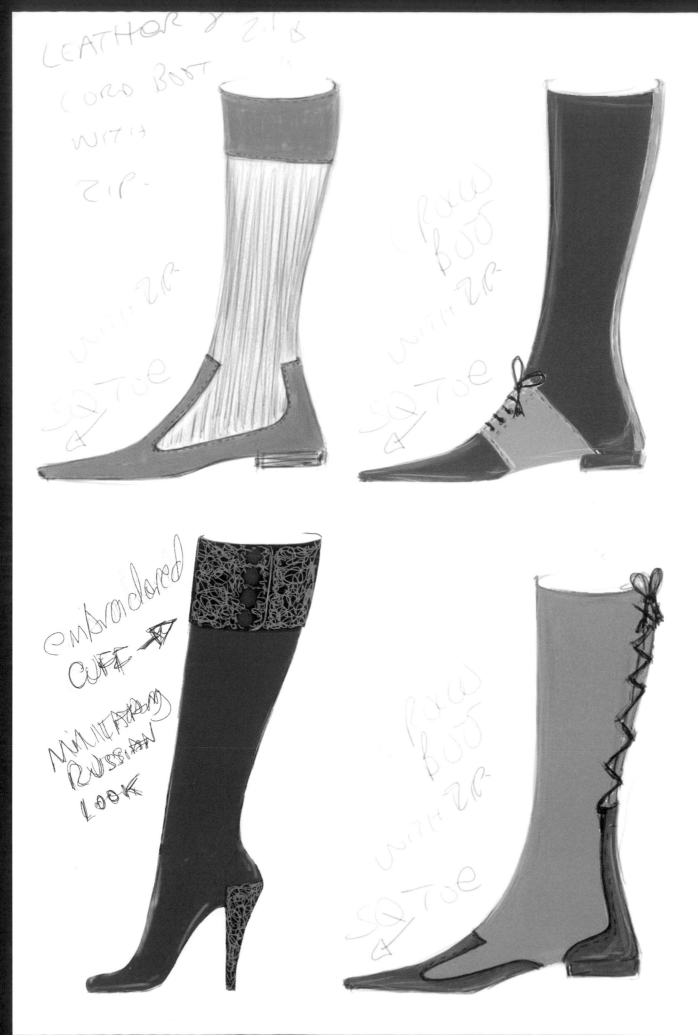

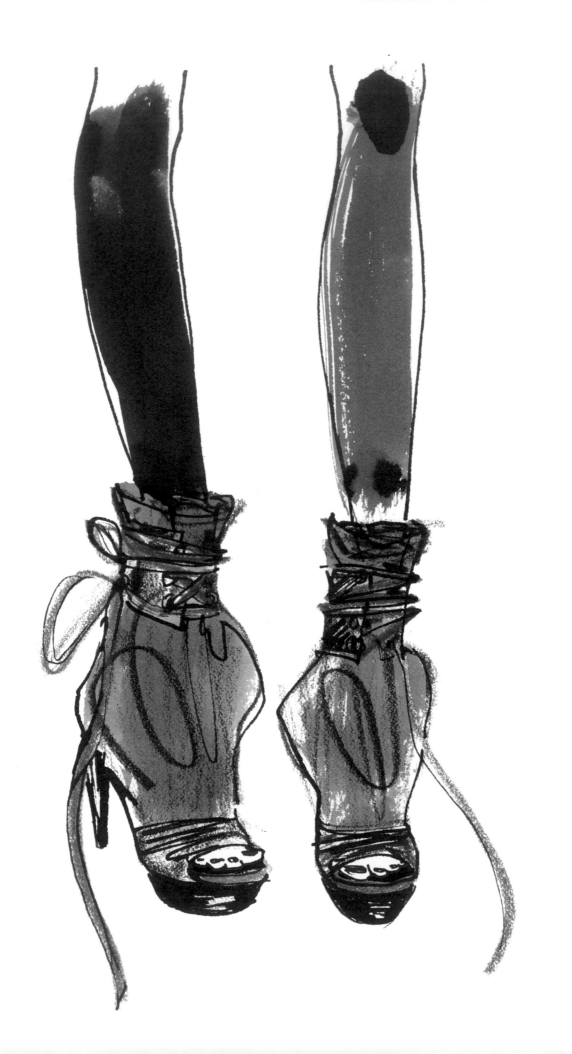

2
URBAN CHIC

SUITED AND BOOTED

Quintessentially contemporary, the urban boot is among the most chic of styles; dressy, classic and iconic, it's an essential part of every woman's wardrobe. Although city slickers have been dressing up in boots for hundreds of years, the urban boot is a relatively new arrival. It was born in Paris in September 1975, when French *Vogue* published Helmut Newton's edgy images of Yves Saint Laurent's classic trouser suit, 'Le Smoking'. Cut in a minimalist, androgynous style, the garment had been debuted nine years previously, when it was condemned for its appropriation of male tailoring. The sleekly seductive cut of Le Smoking – named after its tuxedo-style jacket – is one of the most powerful silhouettes ever created for women; when Newton photographed it on the lithe physique of the Scandinavian model Vibeke Knutsen it had an extraordinary allure. Her pose was masculine and provocative, her feet anchored firmly to the seventeenth-century cobblestones of rue Aubriot as if claiming the entire arrondissement as her own. The high-heeled boots she wore were sculpted tightly to her feet; the stance they gave her was unequivocally confident. The image created an indissoluble link between modern style, footwear and female power, a triptych that remains a cornerstone of urban fashion today.

The boots worn in the 1960s were essentially masculine styles that had been adapted for women. Although boots were widely popular among urban women when Le Smoking was first launched in 1966, trousers were not yet in vogue. Many European and North American corporations had dress codes that dictated ties for men and skirts for female employees. Even outside the workplace, women were discouraged from wearing trousers, and certain hotels and restaurants in London and Paris were known to deny entry to women wearing them. Nan Kempner, a famous New York socialite and early client of Saint Laurent, was refused a table at a Parisian restaurant because she was wearing a Saint Laurent trouser suit. Legend has it that she simply removed the suit's trousers and cinched the waist of the dinner jacket, then strode through the restaurant as though she was wearing a mini-dress.

Stories told by Kempner, and women like her, reveal that boots were a mainstay of the urban wardrobe long before trousers were. Boots of the 1960s and 1970s were modelled after riding boots and military styles, divested of feminine detailing and no longer regarded as strictly male attire. They enabled any woman to step out into the street with Knutsen's confident stance, or to embody the uncompromising authority of Le Smoking in any ensemble. Whether worn with a skirt or paired with trousers, they challenged the long-standing trinity of pumps, stockings and hemline and offered an attractive alternative. Newton's image marked a moment in fashion history when women first stood shoulder to shoulder with men, and when boots, trousers, self-assurance and style created the urban look.

Around this time the traditional woman of fashion began to disappear, to be replaced by women who wanted multipurpose garments with maximum functionality, high-calibre elegance and efficient footwear. In an era characterized by unprecedented mobility, women moved freely and looked for footwear that paralleled the power and independence that was beginning to be theirs. Yet they also wanted femininity; boots crafted with high heels, sculpted calves and delicate detailing gave them just that. Against the newly built backdrop of the modern cityscape, contemporary boots were also curiously nostalgic. Boots, with their long history, resonate with the past. Well-made boots use traditional techniques, aligning new styles with time-honoured craftsmanship.

Throughout the 1970s boots reflected the new optimism that women felt. Women had careers and led independent lives, and strove for equal footing with men. Women said that wearing boots gave them longer strides and made them feel more rooted to the floor beneath them. They reported that men looked into their eyes rather than down at their ankles, and therefore listened to what they had to say. Actresses such as Diane Keaton, Jane Fonda and Faye Dunaway were seen in boots both on-screen and off, and they made boots an inherent facet of the urban lifestyles of the characters they portrayed.

Urban boots may have emerged as a lifestyle choice, but they are also statements of style. Most women would describe them as 'dressy', meaning that they possess a certain elegance or subtle sophistication. They can heighten the impact of business attire, such as a smart suit or a corporate uniform, or play down a cocktail dress to make it more appropriate for day. A pair of high-heeled boots is as easily matched to jeans or a denim skirt as to a Chanel suit, while comfortable, low-heeled styles are perfect for pounding the pavement by day and traversing the dance floor by night.

Opposite:
Boot-wearing icons such as Jane Fonda epitomized urban chic, making boots a staple of many American women's wardrobes, even before trousers were popular.

Urban boots evolved in response to the city, and they reflect the cityscape in surprising ways. Military tailoring has inspired some simple, practical styles, often echoing the boots worn by police officers. Just as art and architecture inspire fashion trends, they also influence the style and construction of boots. For example, inspired by Meret Oppenheim's famous fur teacup of 1936, Elsa Schiaparelli trimmed a pair of boots with monkey fur in 1938. The style was revisited 70 years later by Patrick Cox, whose black suede 'Tara' bootie was trimmed with goat hair.

Christian Louboutin found inspiration in graffiti when working on his Autumn/Winter 2008 collection, which featured boots made with edgy, urban prints. The style of graffiti printed on the boots relates to elements of hip hop culture, created by graffiti taggers who would 'bomb' a train carriage with their work or 'write' a colourful image on a wall. By 'tagging' his work with graffiti, Louboutin anchored it irrefutably to the cityscape.

Just as structures built in luminous glass, shiny metal and white concrete appeal to the sensibilities of fashion designers, so they also inspire boot designers. Both Patrick Cox and Alexander McQueen have designed boots with spiral zips that recall the twisting structure of Frank Gehry's Guggenheim Museum in Bilbao. For Autumn/Winter 2008, Emmanuel Ungaro designed a low boot with a series of transparent panels. The boot's strict profile and streamlined surface displayed the hallmarks of architectural minimalism, while the transparent panels echoed the windows of skyscrapers. Footwear brand United Nude gained acclaim for its Möbius shoe design in 2003, which it later recreated in an ankle boot. Like the shoe, the boot is made with a single strip of material twisted around on itself to form the sole, heel and upper. United Nude also designed a boot that evokes the textile mesh structures of contemporary architecture. With its lateral seams and sleek contours, the boot is more akin to the undulating structures designed by the digital designers of NOX Architecture than to traditional footwear.

The urban appeal of stylish boots has perhaps been showcased nowhere better than in the American sitcom *Sex and the City*, whose characters revere footwear and regard designer shoes as the height of chic. From sidewalk saunters to leafy strolls in Central Park, Carrie, Samantha, Charlotte and Miranda took sleek strides through New York with Alaïa, Blahnik, Cavalli and Choo firmly underfoot. Boots of all types were worn with everything from jeans to a wedding dress, and they often blurred the boundaries between day wear and evening wear. Boots took on a life of their own in the series, showing how a different style can create a new identity for the wearer by aligning her with cutting-edge street style, glamour, femininity or power.

Sex and the City's costuming team selected up to 50 outfits for each show, seeming to choose boots that flattered an actress's physique rather than necessarily coordinating with her outfit. Their choice of ankle boots showed off the calves to make the lower legs more of a feature, while close-fitting sculpted boots flattered the entire leg and made it appear even longer. Not only did the series show that boots have sex appeal, it revealed that boots are about status, mood, attitude and ambition as much as style.

CITY SLICKERS

The well-heeled women of New York are just as devoted to boots in real life as they are on film. Style-savvy shoppers are as likely to browse for boots by their favourite fashion designer as they are to shop for them at shoe designers' boutiques. Manhattan-born Marc Jacobs creates both clothing and footwear that capture New York's edgy atmosphere, famously collaborating with such designers as Steven Sprouse to create graffiti-inspired motifs, or teaming up with artists such as Richard Prince to inject some Manhattan mojo into Louis Vuitton's classic motifs. Some of Jacobs's designs have even referenced the city's glorious past in collections that have reclaimed the nostalgia and retro styles of previous decades.

Michael Kors was born on Long Island and established his label in New York. Known for his classic cuts and his luxurious yet practical clothing and accessories, Kors is regarded as a creator of quintessentially American designs. His boots are either produced under his own KORS label or for his MICHAEL brand. Kors's designs range from seductive stiletto-heeled styles to rugged all-weather boots.

Opposite:
Sex and the City's cast, and Carrie Bradshaw (played by Sarah Jessica Parker) in particular, showed that boots could be worn year round and at all times of day and night, and revealed what a sexy accessory they can be.

Chinese-American designer Anna Sui was born in Detroit but started her label in New York, presenting her first catwalk collection in 1991. In 1997, Sui launched her footwear brand, which is produced by Ballin in Venice. Her boots include comfortable, casual styles, as well as sophisticated, dressy designs crafted in velvet, patent leather, snakeskin and lizard, suede and shearling.

Austrian fashion designer Helmut Lang began designing footwear in 1990 and moved the brand's headquarters to New York in 1997. The label was sold in 2004 and Lang left the brand the following year; it was subsequently re-launched in 2007, continuing to produce clothing, boots and accessories under the Helmut Lang name but without his involvement. Today, Helmut Lang boots continue to mirror the signature streamlined cuts that made the label famous. The boots are crafted with sharp lines and concise cuts that result in elegant silhouettes, and some are produced in high-tech materials more common in high-performance sports shoes than conventional footwear.

BOOTED BRITS

When it comes to boots, Londoners have been setting new styles for centuries. London has long been a leading centre of bootmaking, with craftsmen working in response to the tailoring styles of Savile Row and to the relentless demand for high-quality equestrian goods. The production of all-leather goods, including boots, was regulated from medieval times as part of the guild system; the Worshipful Company of Cordwainers (as makers of fine footwear were called) was established in 1272 to control the quality of materials and standard of craftsmanship. Well-established footwear specialists such as John Lobb, James Taylor & Son and Jones the Bootmaker were born out of the Cordwainers tradition and continue to produce hand-crafted boots today.

British footwear rose to new heights during the 1970s when the Spanish-born designer Manolo Blahnik established his label in London. At a time when women's footwear was dominated by clunky heels and platform soles, Blahnik revived the stiletto heel and the sleekly arched sole. Few designers have created shoes that are as artistically designed or as technically perfect, or that are in a style so distinctive that no other footwear brand could imitate it. In the label's early years, Blahnik collaborated with fashion designers such as Jean Muir and Ossie Clark, then later with John Galliano, and more recently with Christopher Kane.

Above:
Marc Jacobs took the ballet slipper to new heights when he transformed it into a knee-high boot with an elegant, eye-catching design. Espadrille soles support the foot, while the square toe seems ready to propel the wearer *en pointe*.

Opposite:
British designers are known for their contributions to French fashion, and John Galliano's boots for Dior's Autumn/ Winter 2009 collection included ones cut so low that the entire ankle was visible. Boots with low-rise uppers emerged as a hallmark of the season's footwear.

British designer Emma Hope studied shoe design at the prestigious Cordwainers College before establishing her own label in 1984. Known for producing footwear for fashion companies including Laura Ashley, Betty Jackson, English Eccentrics, Arabella Pollen and Nicole Farhi, Hope opened her first boutique in London in 1987, and two others followed in 1997 and 1999.

Another Cordwainers graduate, Patrick Cox, moved to London from Toronto in 1983; commissions from Vivienne Westwood and John Galliano brought him into the fashion limelight. He launched his first collection in 1985 and opened a boutique in 1991. Cox's brand has become synonymous with all things British. From shoe designs decorated with the Union Jack to footwear imbued with cutting-edge creativity, innovation has been key to his work. Cox famously designed a battery-powered fibre-optic boot that illuminated the wearer with every step.

Joseph Azagury first set up shop in the Knightsbridge showroom of his couturier brother, Jacques, before opening his own boutique in 1990. Azagury's boots, like his shoes, are the embodiment of luxury and style. His designs are moulded perfectly to the ankle and calf, making the entire leg look toned and defined.

Jimmy Choo moved to London from Malaysia, rocketing to fame when *Vogue* devoted an eight-page spread to him in a 1988 issue, inspiring Princess Diana to start wearing his designs a short time later. Choo's boot designs are characteristically streamlined and sleek, ranging in style from ankle boots to knee-high, occasionally climbing over the knee. Ornamentation is typically restrained – simple buckles or metal studs – though when the brand launched the 'Bill' suede boot with beaded fringe in Autumn/Winter 2008 it seemed to signal a new direction.

PARISIAN PLATFORMS

Paris, like London, has a long legacy of stylish boots. For centuries, the renowned *bottiers* and *cordonniers* of Paris have crafted boots worthy of their exalted reputation. Throughout history, royalty, nobility and heads of state have travelled to Paris to order their boots, shoes and leather goods. One of the leading firms is Hermès – as the carriage and horse in its logo reveal, it started out by manufacturing coaches and riding equipment. Hermès had been been making riding boots for nearly two centuries when it decided to create fashion boots for urban wear. The firm's boots are considered to be the height of fashion today, not least because the simplicity and efficiency they perfected in riding boots underpins the other styles they produce.

For bespoke boots, the rich and famous flock to the fêted Maison Massaro in rue de la Paix, where they are measured and have moulds of their feet made. One fitting is all that is required, because Maison Massaro keeps its clients' moulds in the archive for a lifetime, enabling them to reorder without visiting the boutique again. Over the years the house has worked with a host of distinguished couturiers, including Chanel, Christian Lacroix, Karl Lagerfeld, Olivier Lapidus, Thierry Mugler and Azzedine Alaïa, and continues to be an influential force in French footwear today.

When it comes to *prêt-à-porter* footwear, Parisian women are likely to browse in the boutiques of established designers, among them Charles Jourdan, Roger Vivier and Christian Louboutin. Jourdan based his company in Romans, the centre of France's shoe industry, but opened his first boutique in Paris in 1957 and began producing shoes for Dior in 1959. Vivier also worked at Dior during his long career, but in 1963 he launched his own label – during the 1960s he designed knee boots crafted in silk and encrusted with jewels, and thigh-high evening boots made with elastic uppers studded with beads. Louboutin had a following long before he opened his first boutique in 1991, and was revered for creating boots and shoes so avant-garde that his work was described as 'wearable art'. His boutique was likened to a sidewalk café for shoes when it first opened, because Parisian shoppers were served coffee as they browsed.

Another shoe designer, Michel Perry, is something of a maverick. He is self-taught, strongly individual and is heavily influenced by urban decay and by British rock and pop music. Perry also cites the decadence of historic Venice as an inspiration, as well as harkening back to the libertine spirit of Enlightenment France. From his boutique on rue Saint-Honoré and his concept store in the seventh arrondissement, Perry launches some of the most elegant boots to be found in France today. Sculpted close to the calf and crafted in supple leathers and soft suedes, Perry's boots are simple, chic and unequivocally feminine.

Spain has long been renowned for its leatherwork, and Madrid has been a crossroads for Spanish leather goods since the time of the Moors. The Moors established a leather industry in the Cordoba region of southern Spain, where they developed a soft, fine white leather from goatskin, known as 'cordovan', which they exported throughout Europe, North Africa and the East. The region became known for leather goods, especially shoes, boots and saddlery, setting a standard for all leatherwork in Spain.

Vestiges of this long-standing tradition can still be seen in the boots produced by Loewe, whose urban boots are made with the supple leathers and long-thread stitches associated with saddle-making. Loewe has long associations with luxury and in recent years has emerged as one of the most creative high-end labels around. Its contemporary boots provide urban women with cutting-edge designs that are loaded with sex appeal and style.

Mascaró was established in 1918, producing leather ballet shoes by hand. Under the second generation, the company has expanded from its base on Menorca to the Spanish mainland and abroad. With five shops in Madrid, Jaime Mascaró makes his presence felt on the footwear scene – popular designs include sturdy knee-high boots with chunky heels and slouch styles, giving a strong retro accent to the collections. Mascaró's daughter, Ursula Mascaró, launched her own footwear label in 1998, and the boots in her collection are typically sturdy and hard-wearing, with subtle detailing that gives them a feminine touch.

Pura López is also part of a family footwear business, established in 1956, but the label that bears her name today is entirely her own. López's designs interpret masculine tailoring in a feminine guise, creating ankle boots and booties in powdery colours and soft textures. Designer Pedro García has both feet planted firmly on the cutting edge of footwear. García opened his first boutique in Madrid in 2007 on the pedestrianized callejón de Jorge Juan. García's boots are among the trendiest in Madrid, designed with a strongly urban aesthetic in mind. Also a family business, Salvador Sapena is now in the capable hands of the third generation. Brother and sister duo Salvador and Irene took the brand up a notch in the 1990s and launched it internationally, designing for women who follow fashion, and crafting their boots in response to catwalk trends. Salvador Sapena takes a creative approach to boots, making them innovative, feminine and distinctively urban.

Opposite:
Paris couture house Balenciaga presented these eye-catching boots for Spring/Summer 2007. Their intricate craftsmanship and striking details made them a central focus during the catwalk show, sometimes even eclipsing the garments they were paired with.

Below:
Spanish fashion brand Loewe designs some of the most stylish boots made in southern Europe. The Autumn/Winter 2007 collection included slouch styles (left) and boots with ruched uppers (right).

Italy is a major force in footwear, and Milan is the undisputed capital: Milanese women are said to leap into fashion feet first. That's easily done in Italy, where such legendary designers as Salvatore Ferragamo, André Perugia, Sergio Rossi and Bruno Magli set the standard for Italian shoe design. Veneto, Tuscany and Le Marche are all centres of footwear production, where boots and shoes for brands all over the world are manufactured by experienced *calzolai*.

A new generation is updating the industry with twenty-first-century sensibilities and collections created with urban women in mind. Casadei began in 1958 and has been in the hands of the family ever since. Cesare Casadei recently became creative director, charging the brand with new vitality as he and his cousins took over from their parents. Each season innovative boot designs explore new shapes and construction techniques, keeping the firm a step ahead of prevailing trends. Their 'Into the Wild' collection featured boots with criss-crossing, lateral seams, while 'Full Metal Glamour' included knee-high boots with wedge soles, rouched leather uppers and a strong retro signature.

Cesare Paciotti inherited his family shoe business in 1980, transforming it into a label synonymous with both luxury and style. The boots resonate with the elegance of period styles, yet they look utterly contemporary. Designs are either devoid of embellishment, or elaborately tailored and trimmed. Paciotti famously designed a boot that could be fastened with a zip, laces or buckles, or with all three simultaneously. Made with stiletto heels and pointed toes, the simplicity of the boot's shape gave the fasteners added impact.

Claudia Ciuti is said to be a designer with 'boots in her blood'. Born to parents who owned a shoe factory, Ciuti knew the industry inside out even before she set foot inside the Fashion Institute in Florence. Her boots and booties are among the most stylish in Italy, crafted in timeless silhouettes that are at once elegant and intriguing. Their surfaces are usually left unadorned, allowing the beauty of their tailored detailing to come through.

Today, boots are the lingua franca of urban fashion. Whether worn in the capitals of style or in areas barely registering on fashion radars, they have a strong, individual place in footwear. The lifestyles of urban women have a resounding impact on fashion; their demands drive and shape the industry. Urban women insist on elegance, comfort and mobility, while also needing to feel empowered and invincible. Boots, more than any other accessory, meet their sartorial demands with glamour, beauty and style.

Opposite:
Roberto Cavalli's thigh-high stiletto boots for the Autumn/Winter 2001 collection fit like a glove, covering the contours of the legs in a supple leather sheath.

Below:
This versatile design from Fendi's Autumn/Winter 2008 collection is made in two pieces. The boots' upper unzips to detach from the platform sole and stacked heel, creating a high heel shoe with a simple 'Mary Jane' strap.

Overleaf, left:
Cesare Paciotti crafted these boots in sumptuous velvet brocade and included leather trim around the wingtips and heels to protect the delicate material.

Overleaf, right:
Roberto Cavalli's suede thigh-high boots for the Autumn/Winter 2009 collection made the seams a design feature by placing them on the front. Crystals on the stiletto heels and platform soles make them even more dazzling.

CHANEL

The future giant of Parisian haute couture had its origins in a small shop in Deauville opened by Gabrielle 'Coco' Chanel in 1913, selling clothes that were elegant and stylish, yet also simple and comfortable. Chanel promoted a 'back to basics' approach, eschewing the old-fashioned frills, flounces and florals of traditional fashions, yet not without luxury. As she refined her ideas and expanded her business, Chanel's unique flair resulted in a brand that was synonymous with urban chic, complete with the handbags, jewellery and footwear that modern urban women required.

Under the direction of Karl Lagerfeld, Chanel continues to produce luxury goods, and the footwear collection has become one of the most recognized lines in the industry. Chanel's boots are a fusion of masculine and feminine elements, usually distinguished by their clean-cut design. The boots, like the garments created by

Chanel, are designed with an element of surprise and a dose of glamour. They are brought to life by the master shoemaker Massaro, one of seven of France's artisanal couture ateliers that Chanel has recently bought up. The work of the other ateliers can be seen in some boot designs – they may be trimmed in lace, embroidered with jewels or ornamented with feathers, fur and semi-precious stones, but each boot is distinctively Chanel.

Over the years, Chanel's boots have attracted a celebrity clientele, with certain styles enjoying a cult following. Boots made from quilted leather and sporting the brand's interlocking 'C' logo are a staple in many urban women's wardrobes. The edgy, thigh-high denim boots are a hit with young fashionistas, while Chanel's biker boots and trainer-inspired peep-toe boots give wearers high-fashion levels of cushioned comfort. As Chanel's uncompromising boot styles continue to be a favourite of cosmopolitan women, the brand remains true to the urban style on which it was founded.

ABOVE: For Autumn/Winter 2007, Chanel designed sleek ankle boots with a classic profile. This pair has a 'fallen' arch crafted in Chanel's signature padded material.

OPPOSITE, TOP LEFT: Chanel used clear Perspex and transparent PVC to craft handbags and briefcases for several seasons before using them for boots in the 2010 'Cruise Venise' collection.

OPPOSITE, TOP RIGHT: Chanel's thigh-high denim boots from the Autumn/ Winter 2006 Haute Couture collection brought street style to the couture catwalks of Paris.

OPPOSITE, BOTTOM LEFT: These elegant ankle boots for Autumn/Winter 2007 were designed with a detachable upper.

OPPOSITE, BOTTOM RIGHT: These boots for the 2010 'Cruise Venice' collection may resemble high-top trainers, but playing basketball in them is not recommended.

LEFT: With their tactile ruched leather surfaces, stiletto heels and their pointed toes, these boots for Autumn/Winter 2005 were among the most striking presented in Paris that season.

OPPOSITE: These sensational boots encase the wearer's legs in silver leather, complete with sleek knee pads that protect the legs.

CHRISTIAN DIOR

Since presenting his extravagant New Look in 1947, Christian Dior has launched *prêt-à-porter* lines and accessory collections that set the style for urban fashion and footwear around the world. Dior's footwear line is said to be the first ready-to-wear shoe label launched by a couture house. Although the House of Dior was founded in 1946, the Dior shoe line was not created until 1953, with Roger Vivier as head designer. Vivier designed the comma heel and introduced the stiletto to Dior's collections. Charles Jourdan was active at Dior throughout the 1950s and 1960s, having been commissioned to design and manufacture shoes for the Christian Dior brand.

Over the years, Dior's footwear collections have included a wide variety of boot models, ranging from flat 'pancake' soles to vertiginous platform heels. Many were adorned with gleaming buckles, sparkling jewels and the trademark 'CD' logo. Dior was one of the first brands to launch boots for spring/summer collections, and continues to design boots in cool, comfortable cottons or silks, or materials such as metal mesh. Recent boots feature curved heels, stacked platform soles, brocade-inspired metalwork and towering heels. Retro inspirations from Dior's own designs, such as Space Age styles and cowboy boots, have recurred in recent collections. Racy, pointy-toe python lace-ups, shiny black leather booties with polished chrome embellishments and lace-up boots with crisscrossed ankle straps and shiny metal grommets are as elegant as they are sexy.

Luxury materials such as snakeskin and fur trimmed Dior's boots for decades, but today they are likely to be replaced with faux fur and other synthetic materials. Latex, vinyl, rubber and high-performance materials have all featured, and technology developed for sports shoes has also crossed over into boot designs. Ecological materials can be found in almost every Dior collection, enabling eco-friendly urbanites to be shod in sustainable style.

LEFT: Christian Dior creates many visionary designs, but also makes boots that are classic, casual, comfortable and chic.

OPPOSITE: Christian Dior is always at the forefront of fashion, and the footwear collection also takes the lead when it comes to boots. Classic knee boots (top left and right) are streamlined and sleek or ornamented with buckles and laces. Bootie designs (bottom right) support the foot just as conventional boots would, while loose-weave leather uppers (bottom left) can make a perfect alternative to summer sandals.

OVERLEAF: Christian Dior's collections often feature subtle retro elements, such as streamlined platform soles brought up to date for the twenty-first century. Platform soles underpin boots with stiletto heels, pointed toes and ornamented uppers, creating a strikingly elegant silhouette.

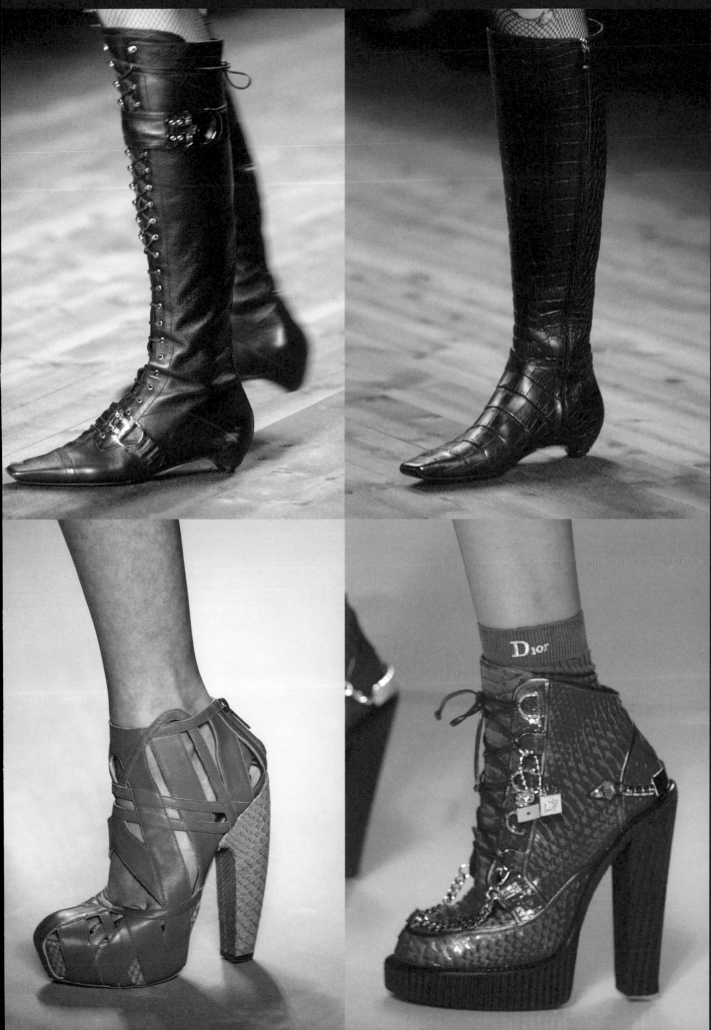

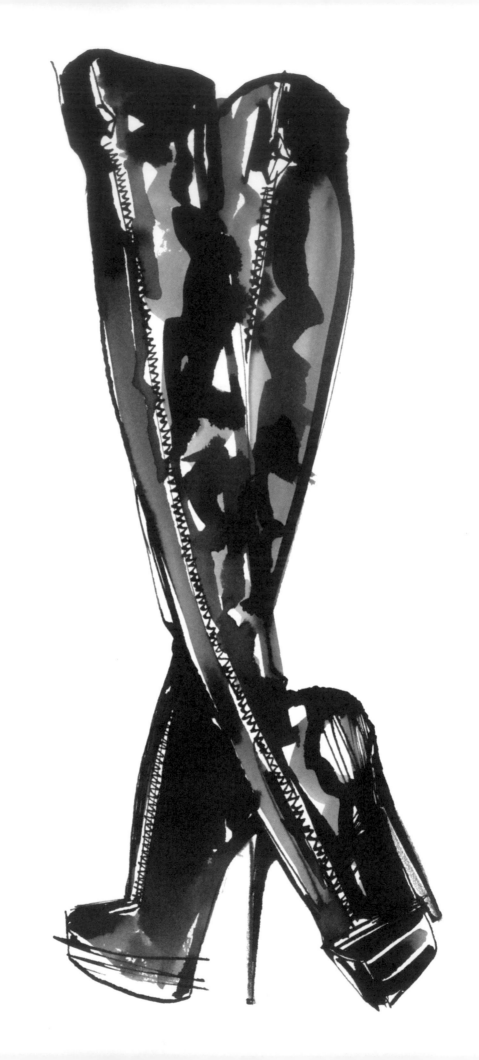

3

SEDUCTIVE SOLES

Left:
It takes a lot to make ultra-feminine model Iman tough, which is probably why the stylist kitted her out in boots for this fashion shoot. Boots can radically change a woman's appearance – as well as her behaviour.

Opposite:
Leather boots have always been part of the rock-chick image. Along with two-tone blond hair, punk accessories and thrift-store garments, boots characterized the streetwise style of Blondie singer Debbie Harry.

Overleaf, left:
The emergence of peep-toe boots in 2008 broke down the inherent toughness of boots, introducing a 'softer' alternative. The surprise of toes peeping out of a boot gets the wearer noticed, making her feet and legs seem sexier and more accessible. The boots shown here are by Vivienne Westwood (left), Pucci (top right) and Givenchy (bottom right), all designed for Spring/Summer 2009 collections.

Overleaf, right:
High-heel fetishism has led to the creation of extreme styles. Ankle boots such as these from the 1890s were made as fetishistic accessories; although they were made for wear, they weren't made for walking.

SEX ON LEGS

Men love women in boots, no doubt about it. Boots can make women look sexier than shoes do, and they showcase the leg in an entirely different guise. Whereas fashion relies on such seductive standbys as the short skirt, plunging neckline and bare midriff to make women appear sexier, boots stand outside the sultry clichés associated with clothing. Boots have an eroticism all of their own, which boasts a long legacy of power, passion and seduction. Chosen with style and worn with authority, a pair of boots has the ability to convey sex appeal more strongly than any garment ever could.

In the eyes of many men, women's legs are not just a means of getting around; they are the highway to their erogenous zones. A pair of high-heeled boots makes the legs look longer, sleeker and more enticing. Thigh-high boots can draw the gaze directly to the pelvis, effectively framing the genital area. Like any pair of high-heeled shoes, high-heeled boots tilt the pelvis forward and arch the spine, pushing the backside further out and thrusting the bosom forward. As they lift the heels and cinch the ankle, they enhance the contour of the legs. The curve of the calf is increased and the foot tilts forward, and the alluringly long-legged look that men find so intriguing magically appears.

Women claim that boots alter their posture, making them feel curvier and more feminine. Boots also moderate the stride; they are designed to ground the feet; the support they provide creates a stance that feels – and looks – secure. In the right pair of boots, an unequivocal stance conveys confidence, even authority, and inextricably links power to sex appeal. In erotic terms, stiletto heels, hard leather and slick surfaces are more closely associated with a dominatrix than a debutante, but contemporary boot fashions include styles worn by both. Shiny studs, shield-like leather and polished surfaces represent a second skin, while leather straps, glistening chains and buttoned clasps bring bondage to mind. Long laces evoke the eroticism of corsetry, symbolizing control over the body. But not all images of booted women depict whip-wielding dominatrices; the boot can evoke a submissive stance, in which passive women teeter precariously in vertiginous heels, unable to master the art of wearing them.

There is much more to walking in high boots than meets the eye. Any woman capable of taking effortless, elegant strides in high-heeled boots has put in hours of practice. She has trained and perfected a technique that coordinates moving the boot with the rest of the body. As with learning to dance, practise yoga or ice-skate, control over balance and posture is the key to achieving poise and grace. These factors create a sense of self-awareness that is unique to wearing boots, sometimes even creating an aura around a wearer that others notice. Perhaps this may be why some men regard boot-wearing women as seductively sadistic; they see their control as masterful, disciplined and dominant.

Women may joke about the so-called 'fuck me' boots that are so popular today, but the demand for sexy boots is something that the footwear industry takes seriously. Sexy boots are intended to be provocative, often breaking taboos and pushing boundaries. Some recent styles show so much flesh that they resemble sandals more than anything else, such as the gladiator boots popular at the beginning of the twenty-first century. The gladiator style sparked a new trend, inspiring designers to reinvent an icon of shoewear by transforming it into an open-toe boot. During the Autumn/Winter 2008 and Spring/Summer 2009 seasons, models trampled up and down the catwalks in a wide variety of open-toe designs. Such designers as Martin Margiela, Prada, Chloé, Givenchy, Chanel, Marni and Jimmy Choo seemed to lead the trend, and others were quick to follow suit. As boot designers pioneered new styles so risqué that the foot seemed nearly naked, boots were the sexiest accessory of the day.

Opposite:
Skin-tight and thigh-high, this pair of boots from Alexander McQueen's Autumn/ Winter 2007 collection lines the legs like a second skin. They may initially appear stark, but their pointed toes, stiletto heels and full-length zips are loaded with sex appeal and their supple leather surfaces are soft to the touch.

Below left:
Flesh-coloured boots, such as these by Etro for the Autumn/Winter 2008 collection, mimic the tones of bare skin, even tricking the eye.

Below right:
These boots from Givenchy's Autumn/ Winter 2007 collection encase the leg in a tight sheath that extends from the toe to the top of the thigh.

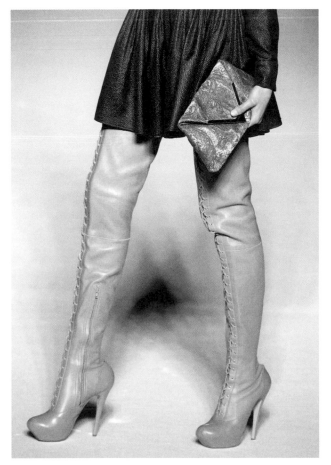

FABULOUSLY FETISH

The relationship between boots and sex has been a focus of psychosexual and sexological studies for several decades. Among fetishes associated with an article of clothing, boot fetishism is said to be the most popular. Sexology studies often cite the boot as a phallic object, but Freudian psychologists interpret the foot and calf to be a symbol of the male phallus, and say the boot represents female genitalia. Boot fetishists have described the experience of seeing a woman's leg tightly encased in a boot as equal to that of seeing a penis penetrate a vagina in pornography. A boot fetishist is likely to bring boots into contact with his lips. This act is likened to oral sex, but with the implication that he is being submissive and anticipating humiliation.

Some neurologists believe there may be a biological basis for the relationship between fetishism and feet. During the 1940s and 1950s American-born Canadian neurosurgeon Wilder Penfield mapped the sensory regions of the brain and identified their connections to the organs and limbs of the body. He administered local anaesthetic to patients so that they would remain conscious during operations on the brain. As he stimulated parts of the brain with an electrode, patients reported any physical sensations, memories and images, enabling him to identify which areas corresponded to which parts of the body. Penfield was surprised to find that the areas appeared to be randomly placed; logic led him to believe that the areas controlling the hands, for example, would be alongside those responsible for the arms, but he located them beside the area relating to the face. The face, as it turned out, was nowhere near the neck. Nor were the genitals between the thighs, but in a region alongside the areas controlling the feet and toes. Neurologist V.S. Ramachandran suggested that Penfield's findings may indicate that sensations can overlap between areas, and stimulation of the genitals may also be felt in the feet, and vice versa.

Boot fetishism is nothing new either; sexual escapades involving feet and footwear were documented in the ancient world. The practice of footbinding in China began in the eleventh century and lasted for nine hundred years. Women in all walks of life had their feet bound to varying degrees; the ideal was the 'Golden Lotus', a foot bound so tightly that it seldom grew to be longer than seven or eight centimetres (three inches). Footwear for bound feet varied, ranging from slipper-like shoes to doll-like, embroidered booties. The eroticism of bound feet was celebrated in the literature of the day: some men were aroused by women's unsteady, swaying strides, others took pleasure in fondling and kissing the tiny feet through their booties. Elegant women scented their boots with perfume and allowed their lovers to take them as keepsakes.

Above:
Shiny black surfaces have long had associations with fetish clothing, but they are also expressions of subcultural style and mainstream footwear trends too.

Opposite:
Although high heels are associated with many types of fetishism, this masochistic ensemble includes boots that are peculiarly heelless.

Above: Traditionally, boots are made to conceal the leg, but this racy design from Casadei cuts away sections at the heels, vamps and uppers to reveal much of the flesh underneath.

Above:
This image showing
a pair of Casadei boots
screams sex appeal.
And, as the photograph
reveals, the wearer needs
little more than a pair of
sexy boots to get noticed.

The first surviving reference to foot fetishism in Europe is by Franciscan theologian Bertold of Regensburg in around 1220. Warning of an impending epidemic of syphilis, he suggested sex with feet as an alternative to intercourse. Regensburg described the eroticism of removing the boot and undressing the foot, which he advocated as a 'disease-free' sex practice. It seems to have caught on in the eighteenth century, when men began to view feet and legs as sexually attractive, even erotic. Richard von Krafft-Ebing, the nineteenth-century German sexologist and psychiatrist, chronicled patients who enjoyed lying at women's feet in order to smell them, fondle them and lick their boots. During the early twentieth century, 'boot-worship' became a subcultural practice widespread among sadomasochists and corporal punishment fetishists. The women involved typically wore high boots with stiletto heels or platform soles – boots crafted in shiny patent leather were especially popular.

Fetish boots came out of the closet in the 1980s and 1990s as fetishism charged through high-end fashion and into the mainstream. Designers dived into the dominatrix's dungeon, emerging with thigh-high boots, leather corsets, studded collars and chrome chains. Patent leather, originally developed for footwear at the start of the nineteenth century, leapt off boot blocks and on to clothes hangers. Fashion garments were made in studded leather, rubber, latex and fur, while racy PVC suits imitated uniforms popular in fetish subcultures. Collections by Gucci and Versace wobbled on to catwalks with footwear harking back to Yves Saint Laurent's thigh-high crocodile lacers and 'Robin Hood' boot. Corsetry was rediscovered and translated into footwear, resulting in designs reminiscent of Mary Quant's corset-like lace-up boots. Thierry Mugler combined machined leather with high-tech hardware, producing a cyberpunk look that made fetishistic footwear a staple of couture wardrobes.

Such designers as Mugler, Tom Ford, Vivienne Westwood, Jean Paul Gaultier and Gianni Versace have always designed for the woman who is strong, complex, yet also feminine. They focus on garments, but have contributed to footwear in surprising ways. They made patent leather more exciting than matt leather, and made such detailing as chains, tight laces and burnished buckles the height of fashion. Their collections awakened ordinary women to the inherent power that boots bestow: high-heeled boots make wearers feel taller and sexier, and more confident as a result. They introduced the fashion world to role-play; women were encouraged to kick off their court shoes and pull on 'cuissarde' thigh-high boots, then go out and explore a predatory sexuality.

The fashion world was also rediscovering black; by the 1990s it had regained its place as a fashion favourite. It had come into vogue in Elizabethan times, when aristocratic men and women discovered that it provided a perfect backdrop for jewels. In the 1920s Coco Chanel reclaimed it for modern fashion, but it disappeared for several decades until Japanese designers brought it to Paris in the 1980s. Footwear manufacturers followed the trend, and the colourful exuberance expressed in boots for two decades began to be tempered. Black boots had been associated with biker chicks, punk girls and goths – women with sartorial styles signifying rebellion and dissent, and who liked black because of its symbolic associations with evil and death. Even as they became a staple of mainstream fashion, black boots still harboured vestiges of a 'bad girl' image.

WHIPS, CHAINS AND BOOTS

As perhaps the most fetishistic of all footwear, riding boots are in a league of their own. Developed for wear on horseback and adapted by the military for infantrymen, they came into the woman's wardrobe when equestrian sports became increasingly popular with women in the nineteenth century. Riding boots are timeless in style, their low heels, comfortable knee height and sculpted, smooth shape making them a design classic. As a fashion accessory, their streamlined style complements a variety of tailored looks. Yet when a woman wears riding boots in the city, her image is more likely to be interpreted as implying sexual dominance rather than sartorial elegance. Mastery over a horse is not easily achieved, requiring as it does skill, strength and sometimes force. Throughout history, the mounted rider was principally a man: the knight, the warrior, the master – all commanding respect. Likewise the modern horsewoman is an authoritative figure – athletic and strong, she rides in a tailored suit and helmet rather than sportswear. The riding outfit she wears resembles a uniform and she is popularly believed to be cracking a whip, or brandishing a riding crop at the very least. Her 'uniform', together with her whip, boots and possibly even spurs, conveys authority, discipline and ultimately punishment, making the equestrienne a fetish icon. When worn on the high street, riding boots may not scream fetishism, but they will always convey strict style.

SERGIO ROSSI

Sergio Rossi began his career in the 1950s, initially training alongside his shoemaker father before moving to Milan to serve a two-year apprenticeship. He established his brand in the 1960s, rising to international fame in the 1970s when collaborations with Versace brought his seductive styles into the spotlight. He eventually expanded his line to include handbags, belts and men's shoes. The brand was acquired by the Gucci Group in 1999, which has since reinforced associations with luxury and the avant-garde. Sergio Rossi has always been synonymous with glamour and sex appeal: over the years numerous Hollywood stars have worn the brand on the red carpet.

Rossi's boots and booties are weightless and elegant, though also durable and wearable; his designs often resemble jewelled accessories more than conventional footwear. Sharp stiletto heels are accompanied by delicate straps of satin or silk, crystals, rhinestones and laser-cut leather trim. Since Francesco Russo was appointed creative director of Sergio Rossi in 2008, the brand's boot designs have acquired a distinctly artistic edge, sometimes even bordering on surrealist. Russo had previously designed for brands such as Miu Miu, Costume National and Yves Saint Laurent, where he played a key role in creating and strengthening each brand's identity and boosting its profile. So far, his collections for Sergio Rossi have resulted in boots that form the basis of a seductive but strong look that gives the wearer a sense of power without undermining her femininity.

Each shoe and boot produced by the Sergio Rossi brand passes through a minimum of 120 steps before it is placed in its box and despatched to a boutique. Few brands are able to achieve the same bespoke-like quality in their ready-to-wear boot lines, but Sergio Rossi has mastered the art of combining materials and craftsmanship with everlasting style.

BELOW, LEFT TO RIGHT: Laser-cut suede leather gives this boot (left) a striking silhouette. Stitched detailing recalls the embroidered trim of historical styles (centre). Booties (right) often feature in Sergio Rossi's collections, revealing the leg while giving the wearer a firm stance.

OPPOSITE: Rossi's crocodile-skin riding boots are crafted with grosgrain trim and dome-and-chain detailing. Reportedly among the most expensive boots made today, they are only available by special order.

OVERLEAF, LEFT: New versions of classic riding boots often feature in Sergio Rossi's collections, protecting the leg and providing a strong base for the wearer. The boots show here are from the Autumn/Winter 2007 collection.

OVERLEAF, RIGHT: When it comes to sexy boots, Sergio Rossi's laser-cut, hand-stitched designs often steal the show. Created for the Spring/Summer 2010 collection, this boot is a one-off.

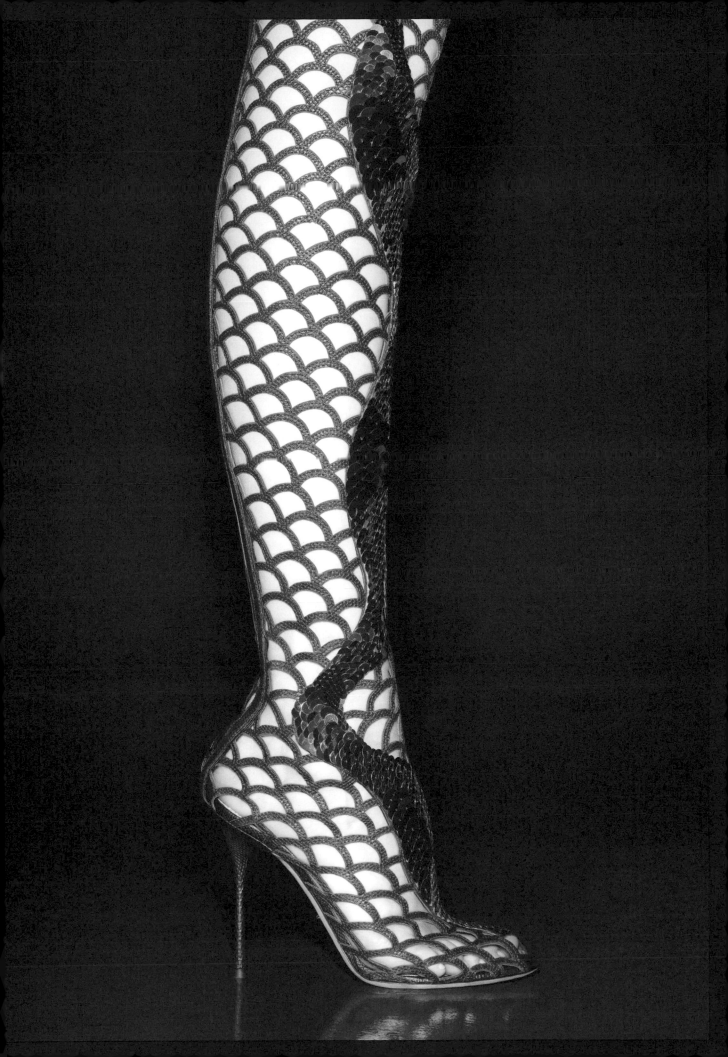

CASADEI

The acclaimed Italian footwear company Casadei was established in 1958 and grew from a small-town enterprise into a worldwide brand. Known for their gem-embellished stiletto heels, thigh-high uppers and towering platform soles, Casadei's boots have a reputation for sexy shapes and attract an ever-widening base of body-conscious customers. Since the brand's international launch in 1964, Casadei's boots have marched across the red carpet on Oscar night, and up and down the catwalks of Paris, London and Milan. Since Cesare Casadei took over the family business in 1994, becoming the brand's creative director, Casadei has expanded across Europe, Russia and the Middle East and has plans for further expansion in North America.

The brand is known globally for its high quality, sex appeal and loyal following of jet-set women – Cesare Casadei claims that each pair of boots and shoes is designed to express a woman's inner beauty and her personality. Many of the boot designs take sex appeal to a whole new level, contouring the leg and enhancing its shapely outline. Platform soles and stiletto heels elongate legs and give wearers additional height, yet also provide a firm stance that underlines a sexy walk. Whether ankle boots, knee-high designs or thigh-high lacers, Casadei gives women shapely styles that make them look, and feel, empowered and attractive.

Casadei is renowned for its use of luxury materials and its artistic designs. Every aspect of production takes place in Italy, using only materials of superior quality. The designs are either devoid of any embellishment or elaborately tailored and trimmed, often featuring laces and buckles alongside conventional zips. Made using traditional techniques and crafted exclusively by hand, Casadei's boots showcase a level of craftsmanship that is rare to find in body-conscious bootwear today.

RIGHT: Casadei reinvented the cowboy boot as a luxurious urban design glamorous enough to be worn with evening wear.

OPPOSITE, TOP: This ankle boot is made with black lace and trimmed with delicate ribbon to create a distinctively feminine design.

OPPOSITE, BOTTOM: Made in detachable sections, this thigh-high boot is a uniquely versatile fashion accessory.

OVERLEAF, LEFT: Details do make a difference, and Casadei is renowned for attention to embellishments and trim.

OVERLEAF, RIGHT: This minimalistic upper is made with a transparent heel, creating a futuristic feel.

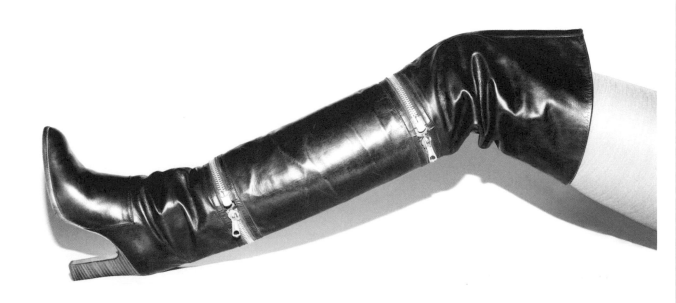

4

STYLE TRIBES

THE EXOTIC AND THE EVERYDAY

The lure of the exotic is a powerful force. Ever since decorative objects made by distant cultures were first brought to Europe, foreign parts have had a dash of mystery and allure for Europeans. From the thirteenth century on, such explorers as Marco Polo began to recount extraordinary tales of fantastic lands where fiery dragons roamed amid palaces and pagodas, and where humans lived in unimaginable opulence. Such legends fired the imagination, leading to an insatiable demand for objects from faraway lands.

From the fifteenth century, explorers and merchants forayed to Middle Eastern souks, African bazaars and Oriental markets, returning with elaborate leathers, exquisite jewellery and lavish textiles, creating a romantic aura around the cultures that crafted them. Jewellery, tribal tattoos and animal hides characterized Africa, while colourful saris and brightly patterned textiles painted a portrait of India. Riches extracted from the South American colonies were sent back home: the dazzling multifaceted rubies, sapphires and emeralds shipped back to Portugal were emblematic of Brazil, while treasures of silver, gold, ceramics and spices epitomized the splendours of Mexico.

Through the creation of garments and accessories from exotic textiles, or from pastiches of ethnic styles such as chinoiserie, eighteenth-century fashions took Europeans to far-flung kingdoms. By the twentieth century, footwear had also made tracks to remote outposts, returning with dazzling dyes, exquisite embroidery and a plethora of leathers and hides. Boots that bear traces of ethnic style are typically described today as hippy chic, bohemian, Native American or Aboriginal. This use of traditional styles in fashion and clothing trends celebrates cultures far from our own.

NATIVE STYLE

Made for one of the world's harshest climates, boots worn by the Native peoples of the far north are among the warmest ever made. The styles known as mukluk and kamak have been worn for thousands of years, and soon became popular with early European settlers. Both are essentially the same style of cold-weather boot, traditionally made with polar bear fur or caribou hide for uppers, and sealskin for vamps and soles. The term 'mukluk' derives from a Yupik word meaning 'bearded seal', while 'kamak' is an Inuit word.

Mukluks are warm and weigh little, allowing hunters to stand still in the cold and move quietly across leaves or snow. Originally worn by Arctic peoples such as the Yupik and Inuit, as trade increased they were introduced to more southerly tribes, with each tribe adapting the style to suit its environment. On the East Coast, boots and moccasins were made from tanned hides of deer, elk, moose and buffalo, while on the Western plains, rawhide was used to create durable soles suited to rocky terrain, thorny plants and rough prairie flora.

The Inuit had looked to nature to create the perfect weatherproof boot. Sealskin and animal hides had to be cut into pieces and sewn together, so water leaked in at the seams. The Inuit used the complete paw and leg of the polar bear to create seamless boots. Observing how the polar bear's dense, multi-layered fur kept its skin from freezing, they also based their boots on a system of layers. Kamik typically consist of between two to five layers, depending on ground conditions, temperature and their use. The layers can be described as inner stockings worn under heavy socks, slipper-like linings and soft inner booties. Two layers is the norm for wear inside the igloo, while four to five are required if the wearer goes ice fishing. Those living further south wore fewer layers, but lined their boots with fur during the autumn and winter.

Although the boots' construction was similar throughout North America, each nation developed its own unique colours, beadwork patterns, fringe, quillwork and motifs. Different styles for men and women emerged, and these patterns distinguished between warriors, hunters, shamans and chieftains. Some boots were adorned with pom-poms, fringe and beaded braiding, or were fitted with fold-down flaps or beaded bands around the top.

Today's mukluks continue to be based on traditional designs, and in recent years have become a chic fashion item. Long before the trend started, Jean

Opposite:
Canadian footwear brand Muks updated the traditional Native American boot style for twenty-first-century fashion. Modern versions like this one are made with dyed rabbit fur and woven braid, and are embellished with Native American motifs.

Paul Gaultier introduced them to the fashion world in 1994 in a collection referred to by the press as 'Eskimo Chic'. American designer Isaac Mizrahi based parts of his Autumn/Winter 1994 collection on the documentary film *Nanook of the North*, combining Inuit tailoring with fake fur and traditional footwear. Ten years on, mukluks and fur boots began to be worn by celebrities and fashion followers worldwide, and for many became the winter boots of choice.

Mukluks took off in Europe in 2003 when Jaime Cooke, a Canadian and lifelong mukluk wearer, launched them in London. In Canada she sourced popular designs such as the Deerskin Thunderbird boot, with its beaded thunderbird design, and the knee-high fringe boot. Several styles are embellished with rabbit fur and woven braid, and adorned with a pair of pom-poms at the top to complete the look. Remaking traditional designs in a range of fashion colours, Cooke adapted the Native American boots for twenty-first-century fashion. From Montreal, Pajar, another Canadian bootmaker, developed chic sheepskin-lined leather boots that also gave the mukluk a fresh new look.

Their popularity was noticed by footwear and accessory designers in North America and Europe, creating a trend for fur-trimmed boots and boots with fur linings. For more than a decade, fur had been virtually taboo in footwear, but the mukluk's success indicated that it was back in footwear fashion. In Paris, Dior designed shearling bags and fur-trimmed wedge boots outlined with metal studs. To many, Dior's dramatic lace-up wedge boots seemed like an impractical choice for winter, but as a style statement they were unbeatable. As Christian Louboutin created a rabbit-trimmed ankle boot with an almond toe and criss-cross straps, Manolo Blahnik hit back with a fur-trimmed bootie that became the footwear highlight for the Autumn/Winter 2005 collections. Dutch design duo Viktor & Rolf also dipped their toes into furry waters, coming up with chic ankle boots fitted with a cuff-like fur band at the top.

The trend for shearling footwear was not started solely by North American brands. A craze for shearers' boots from New Zealand and Australia also took hold, inspiring the sheepskin boots known as Uggs. Their popularity has made a relatively unknown Antipodean tradition one of the hottest designs in Europe. Shearers' boots are typically made from felted material with a seam at the back and a gathered leather upper that creates a rounded toe. Some of the boots slip on like a pair of galoshes, while others have laces at the front covered by flaps that fasten on the outside. The flap is an essential part of the boot, originally invented to prevent the shearer's comb from catching in the laces.

COWBOY BOOTS

The origins of the cowboy boot are shrouded in mystery, but the distinctively styled boot of the American West doubtless evolved from several sources, including those of fifteenth-century Spanish *vaqueros* (cowboys). The conquistadors, like the Portuguese 'bandeirantes' who colonized Brazil, had a tradition of boots with high tops to protect the lower legs, pointed toes to help guide the foot into the stirrup, and high heels to keep the foot from slipping through it. This style, and associated leather-working techniques, spread northward to regions that later became the south-western United States, where they were worn by horsemen, cattle-breeders and cow-herders. The cowboy boot as we know it today gradually took shape, with its chunky heel, slick leather sole (so wearers could smoothly insert and remove feet from stirrups), and an upper that was wider than traditional English-style riding boots or than military boots. This loose fit ensured that if the cowboy fell off the horse his body weight would pull his foot free if the boot remained stuck in the stirrup.

A cowboy viewed his boots as part of his essential working equipment, along with his saddle, bridle and other leather gear, but fashion magazines from the time reveal that by the mid-nineteenth century the cowboy boot was made with decorative top-stitching and leather cut-outs. The underslung heel was already in place and the top of the uppers was sculpted on either side. These stylistic elements, together with other decorative features, distinguished the boot from military styles and other riding boots. Cowboy boots were also made for female riders, but they were still regarded as a male accessory.

Today, cowboy boots are made for both sexes and come in three basic styles: the western, the roper and the rancher boot. The classic western style is characterized by a narrowed, pointed toe, a tall boot shaft that extends at least to mid-calf and an angled heel. The roper style is more recent, made with a shorter upper that extends above the ankle without reaching mid-calf. The heel is quite low and usually squared-off. Roper boots are considered to be easier

Opposite:
Jean Paul Gaultier uses a wide range of new and traditional materials to make boots. This boot combines layers of soft suede, laser-cut leather and mock crocodile to create contrasting textures and interesting surfaces.

to walk in than the classic boots, but are robust enough to anchor the stirrups and press against the horse's sides. Some roper styles are produced with laces to provide a tighter fit around the ankle. Although roper boots were initially made with rounded toes they tend to reflect new trends in boots. The rancher style has a wide heel, giving the wearer better balance than other types. The toe is usually round or square, but never pointed. The shaft is a little shorter than a standard cowboy boot, and the vamp is often fitted with leather straps.

When Ralph Lauren launched his 'Western' collection in the 1970s he was the first fashion designer to show cowboy boots on the catwalk, thereby kickstarting the craze for cowboy boots that spread from the United States to Europe. Collections by European designers such as Christian Louboutin began to feature cowboy boots, and Gucci presented them on the catwalk in Milan. Other designers have followed suit, including Michael Kors, who launched the term 'Sundance Chic' with his Autumn/Winter 1999 collection.

American bootmaker Frye, founded in 1863, has probably contributed to the cowboy boot's development more than any other brand. Frye military boots, in the Wellington style, were worn by Union and Confederate soldiers during the American Civil War (1861–65), and by soldiers in the Spanish–American War (1898). Homesteading families heading west in the nineteenth century bought Frye boots for the journey ahead, and when Western-style riding became a popular female pastime, Frye created boots for women. Today, their classic Harness boot, often seen on the feet of country and western singers and Hollywood stars, holds a treasured place in many women's wardrobes.

Women with a passion for cowboy boots look for authentic models that guarantee comfort and style. Genuine cowboy boots should have stacked leather heels rather than synthetic leather or laminate ones, and their 'counter' (the reinforced heel support) should be crafted from quality leather that holds its shape. The boots should be made with an invisible steel shank hidden under the arch, which is held in place by small wooden pegs. The leather should be completely free of gouge marks or scars, evenly coloured and finished in a soft sheen.

As cowboy boots became a staple of women's fashion, the heel became higher and the pointed toe was made sleeker. Traditionally, cowboy boots were made in tough cowhide, but today materials such as python, lizard, alligator, ostrich, elephant or stingray are also popular. Classic cowboy boots may feature only single rows of top-stitching, but those made for fashion are embellished with decorative stitching, cut-outs, emblems and bold colourways.

STRIDENT STEPPES

The embroidered boot styles of Central Asia are among the most beautiful in the world. For several millennia, nomadic peoples including the Kirghiz, Tajiks, Kazakhs and Uzbeks have lived on the Steppes, migrating seasonally. Each group has its own textile tradition, and fabrics, sewing techniques and embroidery tend to move fluidly between clothing and architecture. The colourful garments they wear, the yurt tents they live in and the boots on their feet are sewn with signature motifs that give each group a distinctive style.

The vast area of the Eurasian Steppe stretches across 5000 kilometres (3000 miles) from Hungary to Mongolia, encompassing Turkmenistan, Uzbekistan, Tajikistan, Kazakhstan and parts of south-western Russia. The ancient city of Samarkand was once its hub, with a central position on the Silk Road between the Mediterranean and China. Though geographically remote from Western Europe, the Steppe region was a unique hybrid of East and West where, among other things, sophisticated textiles and elaborate footwear were developed.

An embroidered boot known as the 'muza' is the traditional form of footwear in Uzbekistan. Originally muza were only for the élite, and even required a special decree from the emir in Bukhara. Today they are crafted from heavy cotton fabric and fitted with a leather sole. The fabric is embroidered with silk thread and lined with adras (a combination of silk and cotton) or silk and wool. Popular designs include the boteh, with its floral motifs in a paisley-type pattern. Uzbek boots are also made in exquisitely embroidered leather and felt.

'Suzani' is a woven and embroidered tribal textile made in Tajikistan, Uzbekistan, Kazakhstan and other Central Asian countries. Nomadic tribes use the fabric to provide decorative dividers between living and sleeping areas in tents. Although the textile is not used for traditional footwear, the beauty and mastery of the hand-embroidered motifs have inspired contemporary designers to use it for boots and shoes. The patterns and colours found in a suzani textile usually indicate its area of origin, with each motif having a name that

Opposite:
Central Asian suzani motifs adorn these velvet boots by American company Edoche. The embroidery style is believed to have originated in Uzbekistan, and its characteristic foliage and flower patterns have been taken up by boot designers in the West today.

can be traced back to its early history. Names such as Starry Sky and Lunar Sky date to pre-Islamic times, when Zoroastrianism was the dominant religion. Other motifs, including birds, fish, trees, herbs and fruits, allude to purity, fertility and healing, while knives symbolize protection from danger.

From their lands in Russia's southern steppe regions, the Cossacks – loosely federated martial communities, rather than a discrete ethnic group – developed a boot style in the eighteenth century that is now considered a classic. Cossack soldiers were mounted on horseback, and wore a type of square-toed riding boot, crafted in supple leather and lined with fur. The uppers extended to mid-calf or just below the knee. Cossack boots enabled soldiers to mount and dismount quickly, stand their ground on a variety of terrains and march long distances if necessary. Yves Saint Laurent found inspiration in Cossack costumes for his 'Russian' collection of 1976, creating silhouettes based on billowing trousers tucked into soft leather boots. The collection revealed the beauty of traditional Russian costume, showcasing the embroideries, jewel colours and rich fabrics worn in Russia for several centuries.

Today, another traditional boot style from Russia is gaining ground all over the world: the 'valenki'. Traditionally made for wear during the Russian winter, valenki boots are crafted in thick woollen felt. Said to be able to resist temperatures down to minus 60 degrees Centigrade (minus 76 Fahrenheit), valenki are the warmest boots made in Europe. Because no leather is required, they are a popular choice for fans of sustainable style. Valenki have been around since the early eighteenth century, when they were worn not just by peasants but also at court. Peter the Great and Catherine the Great owned valenki, as did Soviet leaders such as Lenin, Stalin and Khrushchev. Valenki fell out of fashion during the second half of the twentieth century, when clothing and accessories associated with traditional styles became unpopular, but remained part of army uniform, and are still worn by the Russian military today.

Although the process of making valenki has not changed for three hundred years, designers have updated the style for the twenty-first century by padding the soles and coating them in rubber. Traditional embroidery is still popular, but Russian fashionistas also decorate their valenki with beads, Swarovski crystals, rhinestones, laces and buckles. Even if the humble people who invented valenki could have imagined that their woollen boots would one day be the height of fashion, they wouldn't recognize them today.

EASTERN EXOTICISM

In ancient China, textiles were resplendent, and garments and accessories made in silk were luxuriously embroidered. Items of dress were classified in three categories: upper clothing, lower clothing and foot clothing, the last referring to shoes, sandals, socks and boots. All clothing was adorned with lions, phoenixes and dragons, and trimmed with elaborate appliqué borders. Silk cords and gold braid were made to edge the most elaborate pieces, and footwear was certainly no exception.

Chinese influences were seldom seen abroad during the closed years of the country's Communist regime, but the gradual opening up of China from the early 1970s generated renewed interest in the country's textile traditions. Mao jackets and rubber-soled Chinese slippers flooded flea markets in London and Paris, providing an alternative style to the jeans, sneakers and T-shirt look. When the Paris-based Japanese designer Kenzo launched a Chinese-inspired collection in 1975, the simple, sensuous garments and hipster-like silhouettes started a craze that swept through Paris, Milan, London and New York.

American designers took inspiration directly from the splendours of Imperial China, creating high-collared mandarin robes, silk pyjama suits, jacquard jackets with mandarin collars and sable-lined evening coats. In New York, the Cuban-born American designer known simply as Adolfo was faithful to classic Chinese styles. His Autumn/Winter 1975 collection featured high-collared 'cheongsam' dresses and sleek, body-conscious silk knits. By the time Yves Saint Laurent launched his 'Chinese' collection in 1977, the look had taken hold. He translated the beautiful colours of Chinese porcelain – Mandarin blue, dusty pink, grey and violet – into a chic fashion palette.

Chinese fashion became chic again 15 years on when Christian Lacroix tailored his Autumn/Winter 1992 collection with mandarin-style influences. A few years later, Chinese-American designers such as Vivian Tam and Han Feng revisited their roots to produce a fresh vision of Chinese style. Tam's screen prints of classical Chinese motifs and contemporary icons, which she launched between 1995 and 1997, were an instant hit. Feng designed slender, square-sleeved tunics, jackets and pyjama tops for 1998 that captured the elegance of ancient China, yet seemed timelessly stylish.

Footwear started to reflect Chinese style in a variety of guises. In his Autumn/Winter 1992 collection, Lacroix included platform booties crafted with colourful floral brocade uppers. Their wedge soles were vaguely evocative of Manchu-style platforms, and their sculpted vamps brought lotus shoes to mind. Other designers appliquéd ciphers of classical China on to boots in the form of exotic birds, serpentine animals or mythological creatures. The Imperial dragon, an ancient symbol of power, was embellished on boot uppers, as were Maoist military insignia. None of the styles that appeared was authentically Chinese, but such symbols and accents continue to be popular today.

Boots from the high-altitude kingdom of Tibet, sometimes dubbed 'the roof of the world', are among the most interesting in the history of footwear: made in the same style for over six hundred years, they are one of the oldest boot designs in existence. They are traditionally made from yak hide, with uppers that extend to mid-calf. Soles are usually two to four centimetres (one to two inches) thick, crafted in a wedge shape that slightly elevates the toes. Delicate cloth ankle boots are worn in spring and summer, made from quilted fabric dyed in red and green. Soles are crafted from thick leather, with vamps embroidered in colourful patterns such as the floral 'Songbalamu' motif.

Little thought had been given to Mongolia by the fashion world until American designer Mary McFadden cited its traditional dress as an inspiration behind her New York collection in 1975, a time when her American peers were enraptured by Chinese style. Those who found out more about Mongolian dress were fascinated: although the elaborate traditional outfits seem colourful and individual, each is actually a type of uniform assigned to the wearer according to sex, occupation and status. The Mongols have more than four hundred different styles of such outfits, providing a Western designer with an abundance of trimmings, colours and motifs by which to be inspired.

Throughout history, Mongolian women, even aristocratic ones, have preferred leather boots to the delicate silk footwear of their Chinese neighbours. The Mongols are traditionally a nomadic people who travelled on horseback, and their boots attest to this equestrian culture. The boots worn today have changed little since the sixteenth century, and may even date back several centuries earlier. As with English riding boots, the uppers are knee-high, but have wide shafts similar to cowboy boots. One of the features that make them unique is their upturned toe, which keeps the rider's feet from slipping out of the stirrups. Although Mongolian boots are robust, they are beautifully detailed, with leather appliqués that give them a special elegance of their own.

OUT OF AFRICA

The most famous appropriations of ethnic styles for fashion are those found in collections by Yves Saint Laurent, who was driven by a desire to imbue fashion with a sense of mystery and exoticism. Beginning with his 'African' collection in 1967, Saint Laurent drew attention away from the problematic concept of the 'noble savage' by showcasing the beauty and artistry of ethnic cultures. The collection featured raffia trim and fabric made from African flax, embroidered with wooden and glass beads, pieces of ivory and ebony paiettes. Sleek dresses in African prints were embellished with strings of beads and wooden bangles. Saint Laurent created a thirst for all things 'tribal', and other designers picked up on the trend. Jean Paul Gaultier referenced his work nearly two decades later in his 'Barbès' collection of 1984, which featured elements of African culture that emigrant populations had brought to France.

The work of Saint Laurent and later Gaultier created ripples that spread from couture fashion to the mainstream, and from accessories to sandals and then to boots. Africa is not a continent immediately associated with footwear, but it has a surprisingly long history of well-made and beautifully embellished boots. Owing to the climate, most Africans traditionally wore open sandals rather than shoes, fashioned from tanned leather or raw hide. However, ceremonial footwear was often carved from wood or even made from metal, such as the wooden toe-knob sandals of Zaire and the cast-metal shoes of Cameroon.

The Ashanti, a principal ethnic group of Ghana, hold ceremonies that include symbolic references to the foot and boot. Traditionally, the feet of the the Ashanti king, or Asantehene, are never permitted to touch the ground. When seated, his feet must rest on a cushion, and in case his soles wear thin,

Opposite, top left: Fiery paisley prints fanned the flames of the Hermès Autumn/Winter 2008 collection in this pair of embroidered boots.

Opposite, top right: For her Spring/Summer 2009 collection, Anna Sui embroidered boots with classical Egyptian motifs, like those that would have adorned temple columns.

Opposite bottom: Bhutanese boots are seldom seen in the West, despite being among the most resplendent in the world. The embroideries depict fierce guardian deities and symbols of prosperity.

Opposite:
Balenciaga's Spring/
Summer 2008 collection
was a showcase of
craft traditions and
striking motifs. The
ornamentation on these
peep-toe boots was
inspired by motifs from
North Africa.

Right:
Brightly coloured
African beadwork
is traditionally used
to make accessories
and body adornments.
Manolo Blahnik
married the tradition
to modern style when
he ornamented his
'Watusi' boot with beads,
cowry shells and raffia.

the king is accompanied by extra footwear when he travels outside the palace. Highly decorated with gold leaf, the king's footwear is one of the most important symbols of his royal status.

In West Africa, the leatherwork of the Hausa people is legendary. They craft boots from finely woven leather strips, creating a richly textured surface or bold geometric designs. Designed to protect the legs while riding camels, the boots have soft soles, uppers that stretch to the top of the thigh and, interestingly, a divided toe. The Hausa do not ride camels with the types of saddle associated with Western horse-riding; instead they have adapted their boots to allow them to hold a mounted position more securely. The top part is softened to prevent chafing, while the divided toe allows the rider to grip the knotted rope used in place of stirrups. They use acacia leaves to tan leather, then dye it with henna leaves. The appliquéd pieces that decorate the boots are coloured with vegetable dyes, or soaked in milk to colour them white.

The Yoruba are one of West Africa's largest ethnic groups. Their leather boots are richly embellished with exquisite beadwork covering the entire surface. Boots made for an 'oba', as Yoruban chieftains are called, typically feature interlacing motifs that symbolize balance, continuity and eternity. Symbols include beaded faces that honoured Oduduwa, a mythological king, and birds, which signify female power.

Among the Zulus of southern Africa, famous for their beadwork, women are the traditional beadworkers and decorate leather bags and boots. They craft colourful beaded adornments for the neck, arms and legs. Each colour represents a specific meaning and the beads are arranged in such a way as to convey a message. The beaded boots they make are likely to contain references to love, happiness and spirituality.

Manolo Blahnik presented his 'Watusi' boot in his Autumn/Winter 1997 collection. The boot was designed at a time when the violence between the Tutsi and Hutu peoples had brought the brutality of central Africa into the media spotlight for several years. The Watusi boot, crafted in leather printed with a leopard-skin motif, was decorated with raffia, cowry shells and African beads. There is no tribe named Watusi, but the boot brought positive attention to the continent once again by bringing its craft heritage into the spotlight, just as Saint Laurent and Gaultier had done decades earlier.

Just as he had explored Central and West Africa in the 1960s, Saint Laurent forayed into Morocco and brought it into the fashion spotlight in 1989. By embracing its colours, textures and craft techniques, he showed how Morocco's intricately tooled leathers, sequins, paiettes and beaded designs could be adapted for Western-style clothing and footwear. Mediterranean flower embroideries, gilded caftans, flowing djellabas and heavy rope-like Berber jewellery were paired with sequinned slippers and embroidered leather booties.

The boots made for Balenciaga's Spring/Summer 2008 collection also drew their inspiration from Morocco's decorative arts. Intricately crafted and constructed rather like a sandal, the style evokes gladiator boots. The boots feature black and white zigzagging patterns, and were fitted with straps and buckle fastenings. The detail is exquisite, recalling the intricate terracotta zellige tile patterns and zouac decorations on wood that Saint Laurent had previously translated into colourful motifs.

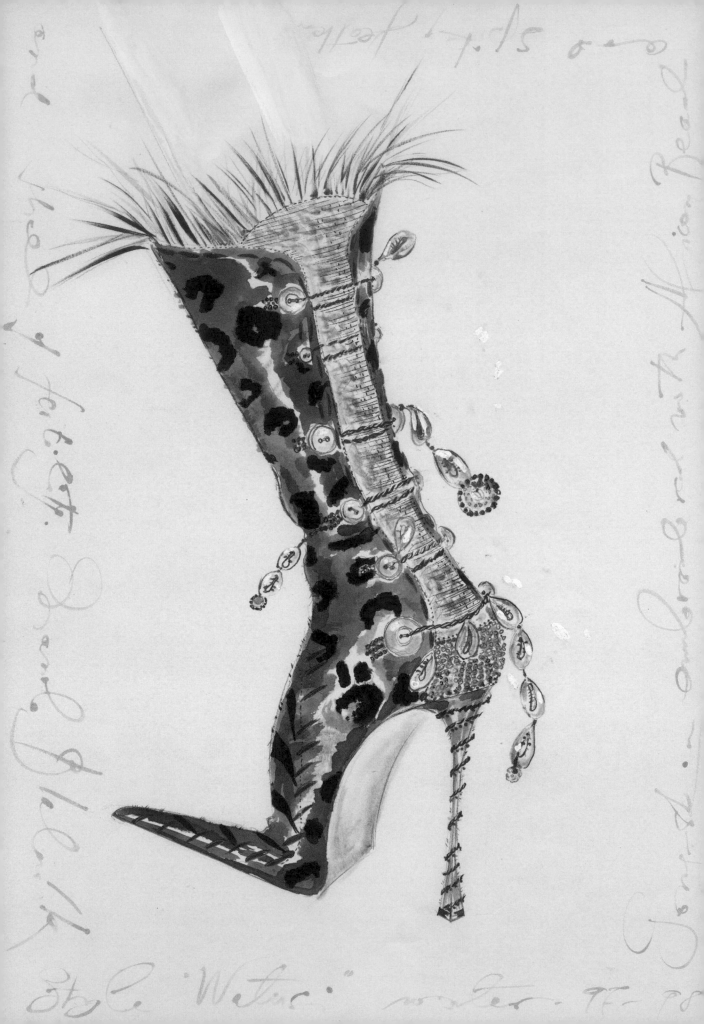

OPPOSITE: Manolo Blahnik designed the 'Watusi' boot for the Autumn/Winter 1997 collection. His sketch shows how a diverse range of inspirations and materials can fuse into a harmonious whole.

RIGHT: The 'Senso' boot from the Autumn/Winter 1998 collection was sketched to shimmer and sway when the wearer moved her foot. The design that resulted was every bit as animated in real life.

MANOLO BLAHNIK

Born to a Czech father and to a Spanish mother, raised on a banana plantation in the Canary Islands, London-based Manolo Blahnik is himself a mixture of exotic influences and diverse cultures. After studying in Geneva and Paris, Blahnik moved to London. He considered a career as a set designer, but following a meeting with US *Vogue* editor Diana Vreeland, decided to take her advice and design shoes instead. Since launching his brand in the 1970s, Blahnik's name has become synonymous

with luxury footwear, and references to his work in television series *Sex and the City* boosted his reputation as a designer of seductive shoes. That said, there is much more to Blahnik's work than sexy soles: he is also acclaimed for his boot designs and for the edgy, often ethnic, influences that embellish his work. His boots have been favourites of innumerable celebrities and socialites, including Bianca Jagger, Jerry Hall, Kylie Minogue and Madonna.

Many of Blahnik's boots are fur-lined or made in animal prints, and bring the African wilderness to the capitals of fashion. The 'Tarzania' knee-high boot from 2009 captures fierce style in soft leather and embellishes it with tribal-like straps and delicate laces. The 'Masai' design was created in 1997 for John Galliano's first couture collection for Dior in response to Galliano's request for an African sandal: Blahnik located the nearest African bead shop, creating a design that went up to mid-calf, blurring boundaries between resort-season sandals and gladiator-like style. The

'Watusi' boot, also of 1997, seems more like a hunting trophy from a Kenyan safari than a piece of footwear. Blahnik combined an animal print with raffia edging and trimmed the boot with an assortment of colourful beads to create an exciting tribal style.

A key feature of Blahnik's Autumn/Winter 2007 collection was 'hairy' footwear, which combined untreated materials with smooth leather. The resulting designs – richly textured and sleekly styled – were described by the designer as 'part Stone Age, part futuristic'. The Spring/Summer 2008 collection was more exotic still, including Ottoman influences and shapes from traditional Turkish architecture.

As well as being eye-catching and exotic, all Blahnik boots are overtly sexy. With their skyscraper stiletto heels and form-fitting uppers, his sophisticated styles ooze sex appeal. Whether simply styled or embellished with feathers, pompoms, ribbons, bows and beads, each pair has a distinctive character that makes it uniquely Manolo.

BELOW: Blahnik boots, with their unrivalled fit, supple uppers and chic details, have always been a favourite of urban women. These boots feature special zipped seams that enable them to contour the ankle and calf.

OPPOSITE: Blahnik's designs for Zac Posen's Autumn/Winter 2009 collection explored luxury materials and surprising designs. Soft velvet and sparkling gems adorn the wearer's feet and legs in a tour-de-force of fairy-tale design.

VIKTOR & ROLF

Viktor Horsting and Rolf Snoeren are the Dutch designers known as Viktor & Rolf, a high-octane design duo acclaimed for their cutting-edge conceptual designs and their imaginative fashion show presentations. Their clothes are often intentionally distorted or exaggerated, and sometimes are based on classic garments, which they reinvent with a twist. Viktor & Rolf have a penchant for multi-layering and deconstruction, and a flair for fun and provocation.

Viktor & Rolf's footwear is designed by fellow Dutchman Fredie Stevens, a close friend and long-term collaborator. The boots, like the brand's shoes, are made in a wide variety of materials, ranging from crocodile, leather, velvet, lace and silk to sequins, netting and artificial flowers. They are characterized by bright colours or bold contrasts. The leather surfaces of their black-and-white striped ankle boots seem to resemble mosaic or marquetry crafted in a labyrinth-like pattern. Viktor & Rolf's use of black is anything but basic: as the boots' surfaces are polished to a high gloss, they offer up hints of deep purple or midnight blue. Sequin-encrusted boots catch the light and take on a shimmering, sparkling appearance, adding a note of glamour to their wearer's ensemble.

Their intricate embossed and stitched boots, nicknamed 'bandals' by the media, are the most exotic of their designs to date. Their perforated uppers bring knee-high gladiator sandals to mind. Made for the spring/summer season and for resort wear, these boots are a striking way to dress up simple skirts and summertime shorts. Resembling the protective sheaths worn by African men and women as they walk among the tall grasses of the savannah, they have a distinctively tribal appearance that gives them a compelling appeal.

RIGHT: Viktor & Rolf are known for surprises, often using unexpected details such as the Frankenstein stitching embellishing the seams on this boot's upper.

OPPOSITE, LEFT: These striped platform boots are as beautiful as they are bold, with their graphic black-and-white colourway.

OPPOSITE, RIGHT: The bandals' contouring design appeals to many, but some women were said to be put off by fears that their perforated design would pinch the calf and chaff the lower leg.

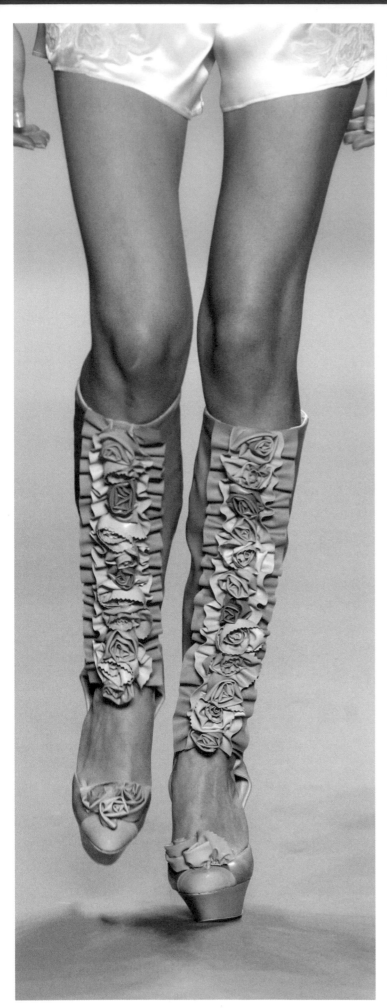

OPPOSITE: The boots and booties designed for Viktor & Rolf's Spring/ Summer collections often feature cut-away sections to showcase bare flesh and make the wearer's legs seem sexier.

LEFT: These sequinned slouch boots for the Autumn/Winter 2009 collection are a whimsical design inspired by the idea of wearing thick socks with high-heeled pumps.

5
SLICK SURFACES

MATERIAL MAGIC

If the boot is an extension of the body, then its surface is an extension of the skin. Our protective layers of skin, hair and nails are shed and renewed continuously, yet they still benefit from being pampered. A pair of boots is no different, its surfaces intended to be kept supple and clean, the soles protected and worn-out pieces replaced. How they look and how we relate to them is a projection of our own identity: boots, like all clothing, provide surfaces on to which we can project our styles, values, affiliations and aspirations, all factors that influence the designs we choose.

The organic nature of leather abstractly connects it with our own bodies, yet leather is at the same time a foreign surface. As it outlines the feet and lower legs it demarcates our outermost limits, representing the boundaries of our fashioned flesh. By virtue of its tactile, visual and olfactory characteristics, it provides a strangely sensual surface that feels good to wear and soft to the touch. Stretched over the feet, leather forms a membrane that conceals and protects the foot's sensitive areas while cushioning it in soft textures.

The material and surface of a boot – whether leather, fur, cloth, metal or synthetic – can change the way the boot is regarded both by its wearer and by others. Boots constructed from latex, vinyl or rubber have a slightly clinical feel, yet the silky textures of these materials are also considered erotic. Boot-making membranes can be transparent or opaque, highlighting or concealing the feet inside. A single material can shift from thick to thin and from tight to loose as it moulds to the foot of the wearer. Surfaces can be multi-layered and multi-dimensional, and designed to invite the gaze or to deflect it. They can be so richly textured that they draw fingertips ever closer, or can be decorated so dangerously that the onlooker retreats in fear.

Although boots are made to look attractive, their function dictates that they be designed for walking in and for wearing during inclement weather. A boot's surface, no matter how seductive, is made to conceal moulded parts and disparate components, and to prevent water, snow, dust and dirt from passing through the flaps or seams. Although new innovations promise to create composite designs that amalgamate all parts of the boot into a single mould, the surface will always exist as a separate entity. Rich with ciphers and symbols, identities and ideas, the outermost layer of the boot will always be more than just surface deep.

Opposite:
Gleaming surfaces add to the allure of fashion. Shiny boots dramatically enhance the garments they are worn with, making them a popular choice for glamorous outfits.

Below:
These boots designed by Alexander McQueen have introduced new shapes and silhouettes to footwear. McQueen's choice of surface materials has taken boot design dramatically forward.

Opposite:
Fur has a long history
as a bootmaking
material. Warm, easy
to work with and as
durable as it is beautiful,
fur is becoming a
favourite with some
contemporary designers.
This boot–sandal hybrid
by Jean Paul Gaultier
showcases the artistic
possibilities of fur.

Right:
In the Autumn/Winter
2009 collection,
Roberto Cavalli included
glamorous boots trimmed
with fox fur and fitted
with gleaming straps.

VENUS IN FURS

Fur is regarded as perhaps the most feminine of all materials, and certainly as one of the most luxurious. The beauty of its natural motifs and the lustre of its pile make it immediately tactile. Fur has a silky sheen and several depths of colour shades within its pile. Its surface changes according to the passing light and play of shadow. As a bootmaking material, fur is easy to work with and practical to maintain. It has an elasticity that makes it easy to stretch, yet it does not fray when used as trim. A single layer can warm the feet even as low as minus 60 degrees Centigrade (minus 76 degrees Fahrenheit), eliminating the need for the bulky layering necessary in other types of winter boots.

Women report that fur can have a seductive effect, and Freud asserted that men found it highly erotic. Despite the sophisticated image of fur in fashion today, fur hides were initially trophies of bloody conflicts between men and beasts. Warriors wore fur hides during battle, believing that the animal's ferocity and strength would be transferred to the wearer. Boots were a male accessory for most of history, and the later addition of fur trim was intended to make them more feminine for women wearers. Could the seductive effect of fur result from a reawakening of men's primal instinct to conquer? Or perhaps it merely soothes them because they believe the battle is over.

The beauty and opulence of fur makes fur-lined boots the ultimate luxury. Pelts from fox, mink, beaver, sable, seal and chinchilla are popular choices for boots. Furs can be dyed like most other organic materials, but the majority are used with their natural pattern and colour. Fur can be shorn to imitate the feel of velvet, which is described as a shearling surface. Luxury designers such as Christian Louboutin, Manolo Blahnik and Marni regularly produce fur boots, while others including Marc Jacobs, John Galliano, Patrick Cox and Dolce & Gabbana have sometimes used fur trim or created fur linings.

While some designers view fur as the ultimate luxury material, others reject it because of ethical concerns regarding animal welfare. The synthetic textiles known variously as fake fur, fun fur or faux fur are popular alternatives today. Man-made furs have been available since the 1950s and over time have evolved into sophisticated fabrics that can look and feel exactly like genuine fur. These high-tech furs are also high performance, and in the hands of top designers they are also high fashion. Roberto Cavalli's faux fur boots are good examples. Crafted with faux fur trim and suede uppers, the boots feature a wide strap across the vamp strap and use suede attached with studs to conceal the platform sole. Animal prints are another popular alternative to fur that feature in boots made by, for example, Givenchy and Christian Dior, who prove that today's woman can be both ethical and chic.

SECOND SKINS

Reptiles have adorned footwear for thousands of years. The Nile cobra ornamented the pharaoh's crown in ancient Egypt, and its image was also fashioned on to royal sandals and foot jewellery. Contemporary footwear has used snakeskin of all types and all colours, with python and cobra popularly chosen for boots. Snakeskin has featured on almost every type of boot, ranging from ultra-glamorous urban designs to hard-wearing cowboy styles. The popularity of snakeskin boots waned after the Indian government placed a complete ban on hunting snakes in 1972, and other governments issued similar wildlife protection acts shortly afterwards.

The python is reputed to be the longest snake in the world, and its skin goes a long way in boots. Christian Louboutin and Prada's Miu Miu label make ankle boots and knee boots from python leather, while Oscar de la Renta produces python boots and booties coated with a rich metallic sheen. Faux snakeskin can be made to resemble any species of snake. The 'skin' is actually a type of artificial leather made by covering a base textile with plastic. The fabric can be made of either natural or synthetic fibres, coated with a malleable layer of PVC. The artificial snakeskins used today can even be inlaid with subtle strips of silver and gold to produce shimmering, eye-catching surfaces.

Other scaly creatures, such as lizards and salamanders, have been popular choices for boots, but in recent years fish 'leather' and shark skin or stingray shagreen have marched down designer catwalks. The British footwear brand Lawler Duffy gained acclaim for its stylishly sturdy unisex designs during the 1990s. They initially relied on conventional leather, but then decided to fashion footwear out of salmon skin. Although the material had previously been used for purses and belts, it had not been tested on footwear before. The designers introduced five styles made with salmon skin, each of them lined with leather and made with leather soles. Fish leather also features in the almost celestial curves and contours of Georgina Goodman's beautiful 'Naja' boots. These look like an art piece, and Goodman created them by combining fish skin with supple calf leather, producing a surface comprised of dreamy colours and textures and soft serpentine shapes.

Shagreen was once a type of rough-textured, green-coloured leather made from the hide of a horse's or an ass's back. The skins were prepared by trampling seeds into untreated hides to create a textured relief on the surface. Historically, the leather was used to cover sword hilts and dagger handles to ensure a robust grip, and to make such objects as spectacle cases and pillboxes that were subject to wear and tear. Today shagreen is usually made from the skin of sharks or stingrays, whose closely set, calcified scales create a hard, bumpy texture. Rick Owens has used the material to create soles for a pair of thigh-high black leather boots, contrasting the smooth uppers with a richly textured sole. Jil Sanders's futuristic boot covers the vamp in grey shagreen, which she contrasted with a synthetic fabric upper.

Opposite:
Designed by Terry de Havilland in 1979, these snakeskin boots rise to mid-calf and taper downwards at the back. A sharp V-cut at the front gives the boot a distinctive silhouette.

Below left:
Loewe has long been renowned for the high quality and wide variety of leather they use. The Autumn/ Winter 2008 collection included exotic leathers such as ostrich.

Below right:
Advances in textiles technology have led to footwear fabrics that imitate exotic furs such as ocelot, leopard and cheetah, as shown in this boot for Christian Dior's Autumn/Winter 2004 collection.

Overleaf:
Although real fur was once a staple material for winter boots, synthetic prints and fake fur are more commonly used today. Fake fur, fun fur and faux fur are made from advanced textiles that have the look, feel and durability of real fur.

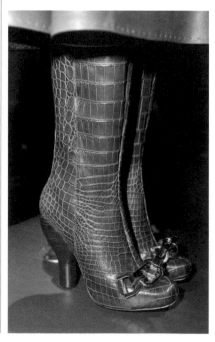

TOTALLY TARTAN

Writing about fashion without mentioning tartan would be like planning a celebration without any champagne. The fabric is an eclectic essential in high fashion, and from there it has spread to footwear. Tartan surfaces can be found just about everywhere, and it is said that the fabric colonized the world long before the British did. Tartan is traditionally a symbol of Scottish clanship and regional alliances, but spread beyond Scotland's borders when the tartan-clad Highland regiments received Queen Victoria's royal warrant.

Since then, tartan continues to be associated with its Scottish heritage, but British designers such as Vivienne Westwood and Alexander McQueen have taken the fabric far beyond its historical associations. Westwood has been loyal to tartan since it was an emblem of punk, and McQueen cut it in radically unconventional ways. Tartan has branded the luxury design house Burberry, and anchored aspects of Jeffrey Banks's work to the British Isles.

Outside Britain, tartan is a favourite fabric of Junya Watanabe and Jun Takahashi, two stars of Japan's conceptual design scene, and several of their contemporaries. Tartan is in such demand in Japan that designers have created Japanese versions: Cherry Blossom tartan is a local favourite, and tartans made in neon colours are popular too. Tartan has been appropriated for boots in surprising ways. Vivienne Westwood designed a tartan boot for Nine West for Autumn/Winter 2006, rippling a St Piran Cornish tartan within a series of natural leather straps, while Chanel launched a delicate white ankle bootie, which was coupled with a gaiter crafted from a dress tartan, in their Autumn/Winter 2008 collection. Ralph Lauren showed it on the catwalk for years before trying it in footwear, designing a rugged variation on a wet-weather duck boot with a Ramsay Red tartan upper for the Autumn/Winter 2009 collection.

RAINY-DAY RUBBER

Rubber can be a natural or synthetically made material. Latex is a versatile natural material that can be synthesized into a non-woven textile or create a coating for cloth. Because it is durable and waterproof, it is an excellent choice for boots. Being easy to dye and able to be polished to a high sheen, it creates the perfect glossy surface for patterns and rich colours.

When it comes to rubber boots, the classic waterproof 'welly' springs immediately to mind. The boot has a romantic history, dating back to the Battle of Waterloo in 1815, when the Duke of Wellington rejected the elaborate Hessian style of military boot traditionally worn by European soldiers. Instead he chose a streamlined boot designed to be worn under trousers rather than over-knee breeches. A leather shortage led to a mass-produced rubber version of the boot, which was manufactured in the mid-nineteenth century. The original 'Wellington' style proved to be impractical over the years and was redesigned with a looser fit that allowed it to be kicked off easily. This model was produced during the First World War for the troops to wear in the trenches, but today it has lost its military associations. The wellington boot has long been a popular choice for the countryside, but today it also has street cred in the city. Wellies have almost entirely replaced galoshes.

A leading pioneer of rubber boots, designer Tamara Henriques has radically reinvented the wellington boot for today's urban woman. Henriques began her fashion career at American *Vogue*, then left to create her own footwear label, launching her first floral boots in 2000. After observing a complicated printing process being used to transfer colourful designs on to children's rubber boots, Henriques adapted the technique to use for adult footwear. Her printed wellington boots have since caught the eye of chic women everywhere – spots, stripes, tartan, paisley, hearts and animal prints are the mainstays of her collection. Henriques has also designed new boot models, including a wellington with a kitten heel and a cowboy boot.

COOL COLOURS

Colour plays a strong role in boot design. Whether strongly stated in sweeping surfaces or used sparingly in subtle accents, rich colours are deployed to dazzle, seduce, unify and divide. Vivid colours charge a boot with a sense of vitality, while softer tones make it more feminine. The emergence of certain colours charts technological breakthroughs, marking a moment when a new dye was developed or an advanced fixing agent was engineered. Chemists began playing a role in the creation of dyes from about the mid-nineteenth century, resulting in synthetic pigments that made it possible to dye boot leather with primary colours that were largely water-resistant and unlikely to fade.

Because boots are often conceived as accessories, the colours in which they are crafted are usually chosen to reflect the main colour trend for a season. The choice of colour may also reflect the mood of the fashion collection or emphasize stylistic details: natural leather finishes or streamlined black boots are typically made to accessorize military tailoring or collections that include elements of uniforms. Leather hides can be tanned any colour, but when it comes to boot leather, it's usually black. It imbues the boot with an air of mystery and foreboding, yet also giving a sense of authority. Black is popular in fashion because it makes the leg look longer and appear thinner. The colour is also highly stylish and has proven to be timeless. Although black is often chosen for military and police uniforms, paradoxically it also cloaks evil villains.

White represents purity and is at the other end of the spectrum. Brides wear it to symbolize innocence; physicians don it to imply absolute hygiene. White boots are considered neutral enough to go with most outfits, yet bright enough to stand out. White reflects light and is considered a summer colour, yet white boots worn in winter brighten the gloom. The combination of black and white creates a striking contrast – it's the yin-yang of colour compatibility.

Red is the most intense colour. It represents energy and can accelerate the heartbeat and breathing, so it's no surprise that it is the symbolic colour of love. Red is also associated with racing cars, fire engines, emergencies and danger, so red boots are likely to get noticed quickly. Boot designers say that red can be applied only to a pair that is perfect in every way, because the colour will attract attention and therefore closer scrutiny. Pink, a near neighbour on

Opposite:
Designer Tamara Henriques has transformed the traditional Wellington boot into a design that's witty, whimsical and chic. These kitten-heeled rain boots are printed with eighteenth-century toile de Jouy designs and fitted treaded rubber outsoles to grip slippery surfaces.

Above:
These vibrant boots (left) for Prada's Autumn/Winter 2009 collection used leather dyed a racing-car red to capture attention as they screeched down the catwalk. The feathery boots (right), dyed canary yellow, were modelled in a 1992 fashion show by actress Faye Dunaway.

Opposite:
Balenciaga's peep-toe boots for Spring/Summer 2010 (top left) contrasted forest green and marine blue with ivory to evoke springtime; the beautiful satin strides (top right) from Chloé's Autumn/Winter 2009 collection have the lustre of bronze. Cavalli uses sumptuous colours to reflect the main collection's palette (bottom left), while Chloé's Autumn/Winter 2008 footwear featured the royal blue sweeping French fashion that season (bottom right).

the colour wheel, has different connotations. Pink is the colour of femininity, and is also considered to be tranquillizing. When the colour is used by a boot designer, it is intended to soften the model and make it appear more delicate. Purple is also a colour of refinement, indicating luxury and sophistication. It is not a common choice for boot design; because the colour is rare in nature, it can appear artificial and make the leather look cheap.

The colour of sky and sea, blue is said to cause the brain to release endorphins that calm the body. Blue is often described as a 'cold' colour. Because boots are more associated with walking, action and attention rather than relaxation, the colour is not often seen in boot design. While marine blue is associated with loyalty and everyday 'blue-collar' work, bright 'neon' blue heralds excitement. Like blue, green is also considered to represent nature. Green may be described as calming, but also as 'fresh'. During the Middle Ages, brides wore green to symbolize fertility. Dark green is masculine and conservative and, as with the colour of the US dollar, implies wealth.

Earth tones, such as brown or beige, are the colour of reliability. Robust boots, such as Timberlands and Uggs, typically retain the natural brown colours of leather, making them seem more of a practical choice than a fashion buy. A yellow boot can be likened to the gold at the end of the rainbow. Yellow stands out among colours and seems welcoming. Although it is considered the colour of optimism, research suggests that it is also likely to incite anger. Brain studies indicate that it is harder for the eye to recognize yellow than other colours, so we are therefore more likely to commit yellow objects to long-term memory. The most cheerful of colours, yellow is not usually a popular footwear choice, but when used for boots it gets them noticed.

MARC JACOBS

Marc Jacobs is one of the hottest fashion designers around today, and his footwear range is every bit as desirable as his collections. He was born in Manhattan, so it is no coincidence that his designs capture something of New York's cutting-edge atmosphere. Jacobs cites Yves Saint Laurent as an important source of inspiration, describing how he 'created this world that was hedonistic, sexy, sophisticated, dark, magical and androgynous, and I wanted to be a part of it'. Surface treatment is everything to Jacobs, who has created graffiti-inspired motifs in collaboration with the designer Stephen Sprouse, and teamed up with artist Richard Prince to inject nervy, urban elements into Louise Vuitton's classic motifs.

Although Jacobs's inspirations are multifaceted and diverse, they coalesce seamlessly in his boot designs, which are quirky, witty and original, yet also easy to accessorize and comfortable to wear. The designs are individual and unique, crafted in every style and stride imaginable. They often feature chunky yet tapered heels in unusual cut-out shapes. Although many of the designs display robust, somewhat

masculine silhouettes, an element of femininity can almost always be found. For example, the addition of a delicate bow may lend an element of *jeune fille*, while classic trim may add a grown-up detail to a playful design. Form-fitted, tapered uppers make some designs sleekly sexy, while daring thigh-high boots with gleaming buckles make a swashbuckling statement. Jacobs's rubber rain boots seem to be awash with style, designed with a distinctive high heel and glossy waterproof surface.

Boots feature in Jacobs's main label, the Marc Jacobs Collection, as well as in his popular diffusion line, Marc by Marc Jacobs. Both have grown quickly in recent years, with boutiques and outlets opening in cities throughout the world. Jacobs's popularity and global expansion has influenced footwear trends, and his boots in particular are often imitated by high-street brands. Today, Jacobs's footwear attests to his remarkable ability to capture the moment more cannily than almost any other designer. As he continues to pave the way for future footwear, fashionistas around the world are starting to think that Marc may be the next Manolo.

BELOW: The boots in Marc Jacobs's footwear collections feature a wide variety of styles, ranging from sophisticated urban designs to varieties that are whimsical and fun. Shown here (from left to right) are a black suede cuissarde boot from Autumn/Winter 2009, a mirror-metallic knee-high boot from 'Resort' 2008, a pony-hide snow galosh boot from Autumn/Winter 2006, a 'spectator' boot from Spring/Summer 2008 crafted in lace appliqué on mesh, a grey leather pant boot from Autumn/Winter 2008, and an engineer boot from Autumn/Winter 2006.

OVERLEAF: Marc Jacobs's designs are strikingly stylish, yet practical too. His winter boots are made to warm the wearer's feet and legs, and are fitted with substantial heels that enable the wearer to take robust strides.

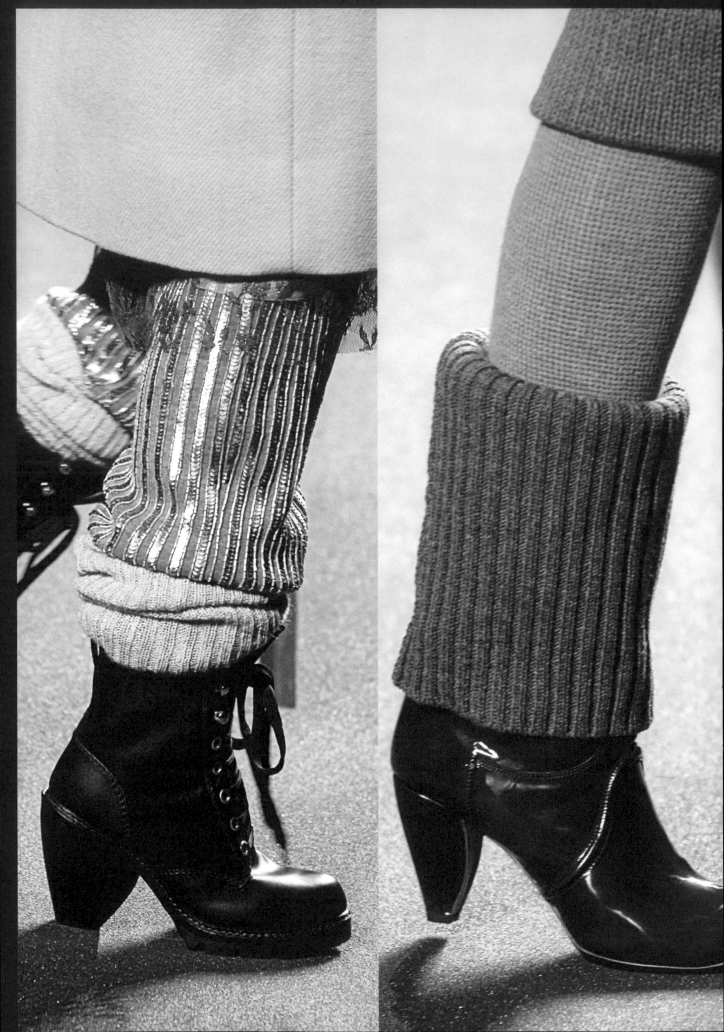

CHRISTIAN LOUBOUTIN

With their iconic silhouettes, spatial extremes, luxurious materials and eye-catching surfaces, the boots designed by Christian Louboutin are some of the most dynamic expressions of footwear today. Since rising to fashion fame in the 1990s, Louboutin has been revered for creating shoes and boots so avant-garde that his work is often described as wearable art. Because his boots are made to cradle the sole, cushion the heel and support the lower leg, veterans claim they are as comfortable as they are beautiful.

Louboutin began sketching footwear as a teenager, filling his school notebooks with designs that later formed the basis of his early collections. He had a following long before opening his first boutique in Paris, having started his career by engaging clientele in person. Louboutin would take his creations to exclusive parties and chic nightclubs, where well-heeled women would flock to his side to choose from among his ready-made designs or to commission bespoke footwear. Over time, his work attracted an international clientele that included both royalty and celebrities: Princess Caroline of Monaco, Catherine Deneuve, Christina Aguilera and Kylie Minogue have all been spotted in Louboutin shoes and boots.

Louboutin's designs are immediately recognizable. His high boots and ankle booties are crafted with sleek heels and streamlined uppers that mould seamlessly to the feet and legs. Embossed leather, smooth suede, transparent vinyl and sleek reptile skins create interesting surfaces, while metal studs, crystals and artsy appliqués are favourite embellishments. One of Louboutin's most striking design details is the signature red sole he uses, a feature that has come to be a trademark of his label. The red sole emerged spontaneously: catching sight of a bottle of red nail varnish on his assistant's desk, Louboutin, in a moment of inspiration, grabbed the bottle, turned the shoe he was holding upside down and began to paint the sole, transforming the shoe by adding the colour of passion and love. On the feet of the wearer, the crimson sole creates a subtle colour flash that women love and that men feel compelled to look at.

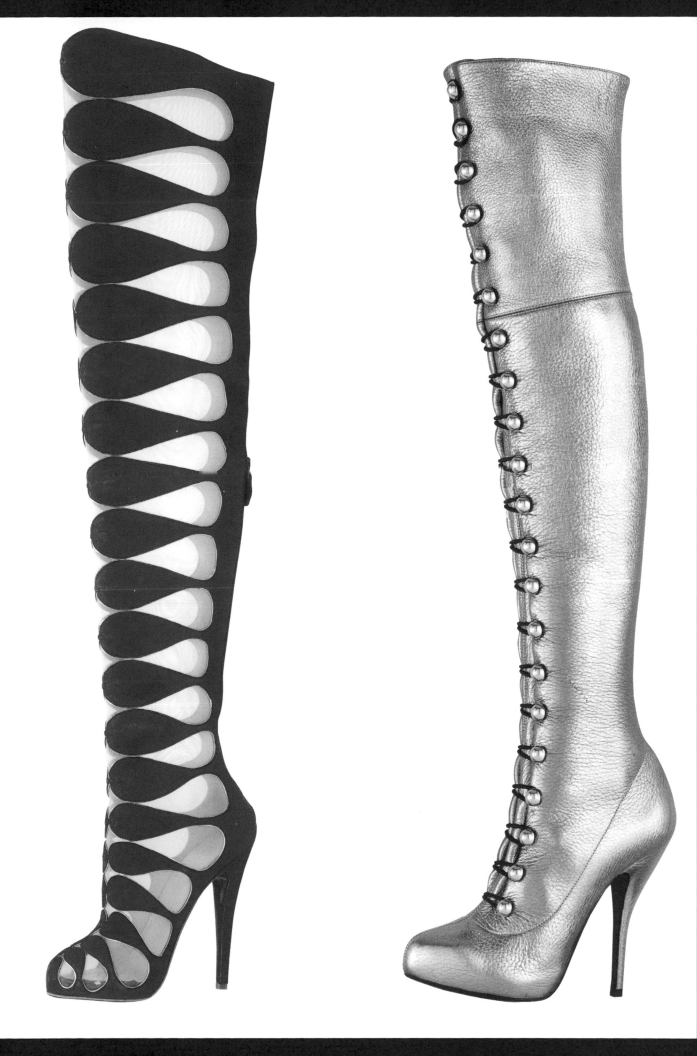

6

STREET STYLE

FROM CULT TO CATWALK

While imitation may be the sincerest form of flattery, it is also the safest bet for a footwear designer. Several decades ago new footwear stemmed from high fashion and trickled down into the high street, where certain vintage models later became popular among cult groups. It is true that the mainstream footwear industry takes its lead from high-end designers, yet the most enduring designs have often come from the bottom up. Remaking a boot style that already has street cred is a guarantee that it will stick around longer than something born out of a transient catwalk fad. Recreating street style is akin to copying a historical boot; both have a track record of authenticity and longevity that new designs usually lack.

Few of the fashions worn today started in the grand interiors of Paris's couture houses, even though that is where many of the world's top designers are based. The street is said to be the stage on which new fashion is forged, and it is where many of today's leading designers find their inspiration. Boots are as indistinguishable from street style as couture is from Paris fashion – where, paradoxically, many of the boots worn on its prestigious catwalks are styles that originated on the street.

The subcultures that emerged from the music scene of the 1970s had distinctive sartorial styles. Although the fashion world was initially dismissive of beatniks, rockabillies, punk rockers and new romantics, their distinctive dress styles proved to be more than just fleeting fads. Over time, street fashions came to be seen as just the tip of the subcultural iceberg, with cult fashion looks being the visible evidence of the ideals, aspirations and influences that unite the members of a style tribe. Street styles express the individuality and personal liberty that have come to be defining features of our age, imbuing fashion with a greater sense of freedom.

Boots with currency as cult favourites were once signifiers of 'them' and 'us', but today fashion has blurred those boundaries. While the nonconformist boots that implied rebellion and dissent were once outside the parameters of mainstream footwear, they are now the very height of chic. The boots worn by rebels such as goths, punks and biker chicks challenged and toppled the footwear hierarchy. Thanks to them, the fashion world is more open to street styles, and their cult boots are as likely to leave tracks on the catwalks as they are on the sidewalk.

Opposite:
American singer-songwriter Tweet is the epitome of street style. Boots are a key part of her tough-girl image, giving her a stance that is stylish, confident and chic.

Below:
Chloé revived a cult classic for their Autumn/Winter 2008 collection, updating the combat boot with a sculpted platform sole and stylish stitching.

Female punks were rebellious to the core, challenging stereotypical images of women by creating styles that were deeply shocking at the time. The punk movement exploded in the late 1970s and encouraged cult women to transform their clothing into symbols of political dissent. Black drainpipe jeans, tartan bondage trousers and ripped tights were worn with big chunky boots. Delicate garments were sourced second-hand, only to be shredded and slashed; rocker jackets and customized blazers were studded, painted and pierced, and brightly dyed hair was theatrically combed into spikes. Dog collars and S&M cuff restraints were used as jewellery, worn together with spike bracelets, safety pins, studs and chains.

Leather, rubber and shiny surfaces were popular choices for clothing and footwear alike. Lace-up boots were the mainstay of punk fashion, and Dr. Martens were usually the brand of choice. Military boots, motorcycle boots and steel-toed combat boots were also worn, and like the rest of the punk wardrobe, they looked rough and ready. Brand-new boots were seldom bought, and old boots in need of repair were stapled together or wrapped with tape. Boots were customized with spray paint or embellished with a marker pen. They also featured rows of spikes, randomly placed studs, safety pins, buttons, badges and jewellery. And if that wasn't flash enough, some punks even adorned their boots with bandanas, chains or studded leather bands.

Elements of punk style became high fashion in the hands of Vivienne Westwood, whose fetishistic platform shoes, studded footwear and pirate boots are still popular today. Alexander McQueen also had a lifelong fascination with punk, and this inspired some of his edgiest footwear. McQueen designed steel-toed boots with streamlined metal points that referenced the robust punk versions, and a chic ankle bootie trimmed with Dr. Martens-style stitching that was draped with layers of mesh-like tulle. He also took the Union Jack, a signature punk emblem, and stretched it across the surface of a shiny bootie with a sleek stiletto heel. Sonia Rykiel has also explored the power of punk. Rykiel streamlined the punk's characteristic black platform and fitted it with five brass buckles, then pinned them in place using metal badges.

Opposite:
Singer Gwen Stefani, renowned for the outfits she wore on stage with the band No Doubt, launched her own clothing line in 2003 when she went solo. Her eclectic suits, high-rise hot pants and couture creations are almost always paired with boots, which are often as daring as the clothes she wears.

Below:
Subcultural styles have long influenced leading fashion designers, For Autumn/Winter 2008, Gucci presented this beautifully studded boot inspired by 1980s punk style.

GOTH GLAMOUR

Whoever said Goth was dead was right. The style has a dark history, born out of images of death, destruction and decay. It emerged from eighteenth-century Gothic horror literature and later from 'thriller' literature and vampire cinema. As Goth embraces the powers of terror and erotic macabre, the style symbolizes death, the devil, defiance, night and nihilism, associations that are epitomized by the meanings and moods associated with the colour black. Goth clothing and footwear have made the Gothic an ideal symbol of decadence and rebellion, and an ever-widening subculture continues to form today.

Goth is popularly associated with rock musicians, black-clad teenagers and Japanese hipsters, but as a fashion trend it goes far beyond cult style. Just as elements of punk resonate with both fashion and footwear designers, so too does the edgy Goth look. In the nineteenth century icons such as Byron, Baudelaire and Beau Brummell revolutionized men's fashion through their Gothic cuts, black clothing and Romantic style. In the early years of silent film, the American actress Theda Bara and the French actress Musidora played tragic femme fatale characters in Gothic settings, such as labyrinths, ruined castles and churchyards. Their costumes rendered a sense of dark glamour that has resurfaced in contemporary fashions: Olivier Theyskens presented a Goth-inspired collection in Paris in 1997, the same year that Anna Sui showed her Goth collection in New York. London-based British designer Gareth Pugh has been acclaimed for his edgy Gothic glamour collections ever since he started in 2005. Stylistic elements ranging from Victorian mourning dress, veils and masks to black lace and jet jewellery have influenced Pugh's work.

Every girl goth covets a pair of black lace-up hobnail boots, with ten pairs of eyelets or more. Valentino's lace-like laser-cut ankle boots combine Victorian styling with the illusion of a black lace surface. McQueen designed a pair of boots crafted in black jet from heel to toe, creating a sparkling surface with a dark lustre. Goths treat boots like holy relics, customizing and adorning them with memento mori such as skulls, skeletons, hellfire and other symbols of mortality. While most women are running around in conventional footwear, goth girls are wearing decadence, deathly romanticism and dark glamour on their feet.

Above and opposite: Roberto Cavalli has often included an aspect of period elegance in his boot designs. This simple black ankle boot (above) is studded with gold-coloured rivets, bringing late Victorian Gothic to mind. This riveted boot (opposite) is paired with gaiters made with eyelet-like detailing, which echo the Victoriana style popular among Goth enthusiasts.

BIKER BABES

When French singer Françoise Hardy was photographed astride a motorcycle in 1969, she launched a look that appealed to women around the world. Dressed in black leather clothing and biker boots, Hardy portrayed a beautiful bad girl dangerously claiming the streets as her own. Marlon Brando had struck a similar pose 15 years earlier when he played a cool rebel outlaw in *The Wild One*. The film portrayed gangs of handsome motorcycle vigilantes that menaced the city streets. The slick outfits they wore were pieced together from old costumes made for military films and Western epics, but they had a profound influence on men and women's fashion. The characters' so-called 'biker' jackets were military-issue, worn by bomber pilots in the First and Second World Wars. Their leather chaps, wide belts and gun holsters had been made for cowboys, and their heavy boots, once protective wear for industrial workers, were fitted with straps and buckles across the instep, which recalled the straps used to attach a spur.

Biker boots give women an unmistakably tough image. The reinforced leather parts shield the legs from the heat of the engine and exhaust pipe, and their thick soles protect the feet when they drag along the surface of the road. Like cowboy boots, they symbolize individual freedom and breaking rules, but when worn by motorcycle cops they connote the authority of law and order. The boot's streamlined shape, with its elevated heel and shapely toe, is a flattering choice for jeans, flared trousers and skirts. Biker boots are an essential part of street style, yet are now considered classic enough to suit most fashionable looks.

Almost all boots with buckles and straps reference biker gear. Chanel remade them into a high-fashion accessory when she strapped three buckles along the top and fixed her logo to the toe and upper. Ralph Lauren's version remade them in their original guise, but streamlined the upper and brought it up to knee height. Patrick Cox's black leather 'Xena' boot is knee-high with padded motorcycle stitching around the knee and heel: the name may reference a character of fiction, but the boots give the wearer real style.

Opposite:
American photographer Lee Miller was one of the first women to be photographed in combat boots. After the war, Miller bathed in Hitler's own home. She placed a portrait of Hitler beside the bath and her wartime combat boots on the floor in front of it.

Left:
For the Autumn/Winter 2006 collection, Christian Dior appropriated the biker boot for women's wear by giving it a stylish platform heel and a knee-length upper.

Overleaf, left:
Viktor & Rolf took the biker boot to new heights in their Autumn/Winter 2009 collection. Anchored to a platform sole, the upper rises to the knee and is fitted with wide leather straps.

Overleaf, right:
French singer Françoise Hardy was the ultimate biker babe, photographed here on the streets of Paris in the 1960s.

COMBAT BEAUTIES

Boots can be comfortable, durable and practical, yet still look great. The regulation-issue leather lace-ups worn by American and German soldiers during the Second World War evolved to have a cult status after the war was over. Since then, combat boots have influenced footwear on many levels, ranging from design and durability to comfort and style. The combat boots made by the military were usually shod with hobnails and constructed with metal plates in the heel and toe. In the 1960s and 1970s, they became emblematic of subcultural style as they were adopted by skinheads, rockers and punks. Out of those movements they migrated into mainstream fashion, and from there, became popular for women too.

The biggest innovations in combat boots were engineered by Klaus Maertens, a German army doctor active during the war. Maertens injured his ankle and found that his military-issue combat boots were too uncomfortable for his injured foot. While on leave, he redesigned the boots with soft leather uppers and air-padded soles. When the war ended, Maertens set up a footwear business and manufactured the soles from discarded rubber found on Luftwaffe airfields. The comfortable soles were a big hit, and the boots became a popular choice for men and women. The style took off internationally when a British shoe company acquired the rights to manufacture the shoes in the United Kingdom. They anglicized the name, reshaped the heel, added the boot's signature yellow stitching and trademarked the soles as AirWair.

The first British version of the Dr. Martens boot came out in 1960. The boot was an eight-eyelet, cherry-red design crafted in Nappa leather. It was immediately popular among postmen, police officers, engineers and factory workers. By the late 1960s, skinheads started wearing them and by the end of the 1970s they were the favourite footwear of punks. Since then, Dr. Martens have become an iconic footwear design, characterized by vivid colours and trendy motifs, as well as the ever-present classic black. They have also influenced mainstream footwear in a variety of ways, making robust, visible stitching popular, introducing air-cushioned soles to everyday shoes and bringing the rounded toe back into boot fashion. As combat boots evolve into new chic styles today, it's no surprise that they are more popular in peacetime than they ever were in war.

Opposite and right: Launched in Autumn/Winter 2009, Jean Paul Gaultier's collaboration with Dr. Martens resulted in some exciting new designs, including thigh-high patent-leather boots (opposite) and laser-cut uppers that resemble a mesh (right).

JEAN PAUL GAULTIER

Parisian designer Jean Paul Gaultier has long been known as the *enfant terrible* of French fashion. His eager appropriation of subcultural symbols has made his label a favourite of edgy urbanites, but he also has a loyal following of couture clientele. Gaultier was among the first to inject elements of street style into haute couture, inverting the widely held truism that street-fashion styles were filtered-down versions of couture designs, and had trickled down from 'above'. Gaultier retained the formal characteristics of couture, yet he imbued

his lines with elements reflecting every-day urban life. Although the majority of his couture clients would have eschewed the idea of getting a tattoo or a body piercing, many happily acquired them in the form of garments embellished with tribal designs and metallic decorations.

Gaultier's footwear collection has had a huge impact on the rest of the industry. More than any other designer, Gaultier has understood the significant role that boots can play in a woman's wardrobe and the tough image that street-style boots can create. Yet he often chooses to tone down rough-and-ready appeal, opting instead for sleek designs that are more about elegance than attitude. The full extent of Gaultier's boot designs can be seen in three footwear collections: his own couture and ready-to-wear lines feature boots each season, as does his line for the French leather-goods company Hermès, which appointed Gaultier creative director in 2003.

A collaboration with the Dr. Martens brand in 2008 resulted in a new boot style

based on one of the company's existing designs. Many of Dr. Martens' styles are unisex – a perfect match for Gaultier's penchant for androgynous looks and ungendered clothing. Lasers were used to cut away a diamond pattern in the side of Dr. Martens' classic 14-hole model, creating a web-like motif. Launched in autumn 2009, the boot was produced in black or white, becoming a favourite with street kids and fashionistas alike.

BELOW: Gaultier's Autumn/Winter 2007 collection was acclaimed for its intricate detailing, and the design details evident in the boot styles were equally stunning.

OPPOSITE: These sporty boots from Gaultier's Spring/Summer 2008 collection combine the efficiency of a sports boot with the sophistication of stiletto heels.

OVERLEAF, LEFT: Gaultier's edgy styles have always been described as

empowering. This archive image from the Autumn/Winter 1987 collection shows a softly feminine silhouette grounded firmly in a pair of sturdy boots.

OVERLEAF, RIGHT: Gaultier's Autumn/Winter 2009 collection was described as highly masochistic: face masks, bondage chains and leather restraints injected fetishistic overtones. The straps and chains on these elegant boots subtly reflected the overall mood of the collection.

ROBERTO CAVALLI

The Italian fashion brand Roberto Cavalli is innovative and experimental, but it never fails to deliver some of the most luxurious designs produced in Italy today. The brand was established in the early 1970s, when Cavalli invented a new method for printing on leather and found a way to create elaborate patchworks made from different materials. Cavalli's know-how was soon in demand by leading fashion houses, and commissions from the likes of Hermès and Pierre Cardin gave him the confidence to establish his own label. It was an overnight success and the luxury fabrics, precious furs, jewel appliqué and supple leathers he used soon became his trademark.

Against this background of opulence, Cavalli's associations with street style may not be immediately apparent. Inspired by the faded denim of rock-and-roll style, he developed a method for making stone-washed jeans in 1994. Biker influences also infiltrated his footwear collection – produced collaboratively with Vicini – inspiring black leather boots with 'hardware' buckles, industrial zips and wide straps. Ankle boots encrusted with metal studs seem like high-fashion memorials to punk style, giving Cavalli women a streetwise allure.

Recent collections have included styles reflecting the Goth trend sweeping through virtually every aspect of noughties fashion. Cavalli's sleek, black leather ankle boots are sculpted to the feet and recall the shape of Balmorals. Trimmed with gleaming metal rivets, they ooze the dark glamour characteristic of high-end Goth style.

PREVIOUS PAGE, LEFT:
Roberto Cavalli
encourages women to
leap into fashion feet
first. Designs like this one
are so striking that they
elevate footwear beyond
the accessories category,
inspiring women to buy
garments that show off
their boots rather than
the other way around.

**PREVIOUS PAGE,
RIGHT:** Over the years,
Roberto Cavalli's boots
have gained a reputation
for being statements of
style. Most women would
describe them as 'dressy',
meaning that they possess
a certain elegance or
subtle sophistication.

OPPOSITE: These
thigh-high boots from
the Autumn/Winter 2003
collection cut a striking
silhouette as they encase
the countours of the leg in
a glove-like sheath.

BELOW LEFT: Cavalli's
collections often include
luxury materials such as
fur, as shown with these
winter warmers.

BELOW RIGHT: Sleek
suede sheaths with eyelet
details are seamlessly
combined with
streamlined booties
to create the effect
of high-lacing boots.

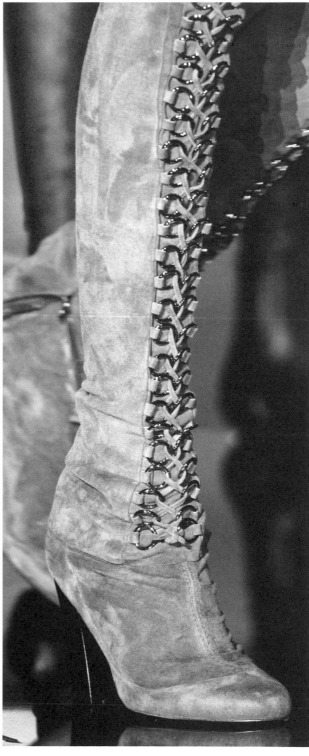

7

WARRIOR WOMEN

PLATFORMS OF POWER

Women have been warriors for thousands of years. Bloodthirsty female revolutionaries are known to have fought alongside men on ancient battlegrounds, and others quietly took up arms and defended their lands when the men were away. In the first century AD the queen of the Britons, Boudicca, led an uprising against the Romans; fourteen centuries later Joan of Arc led French soldiers into battle against the English. In the seventeenth century, the African kingdom of Dahomey deployed a legion of female soldiers to invade cities and conquer them for the king. The Amazon river was so named after the Spanish explorer Francisco de Orellana reported attacks by a fierce tribe of spear-wielding women who were reminiscent of the mythical female warriors chronicled by the ancient Greeks. And though rare in the Roman world, female gladiators did exist.

A burial mound attributed to the ancient Scythians contained the remains of a woman buried in full battle dress. Her boots were typical of the Scythians, and at her feet was an assortment of weapons and war trophies. Her leg bones were significantly bowed, suggesting that she had spent most of her life on horseback, and the arrowhead lodged in her chest indicates that she probably died in battle. The Scythians' lands bordered ancient Greece at the spot where the legendary Amazons were said to live, so it is possible that this ancient female warrior may have been an Amazon, or part of a tribe of female warriors from which the accounts of the Amazons perhaps stemmed. Her grave is certainly evidence that weaponized women flourished in the ancient world.

Neither fashion nor footwear has ever forgotten women's warrior roots. When designers use military tailoring to make clothes for women, they create strict styles that men take seriously. When Miuccia Prada was asked about her fascination with military styling, she explained to *Women's Wear Daily* that she was 'tired of all that passive, sweet femininity. We women should go back to some strength.' Prada's statement explains why boots resonate with contemporary women, who have long sought respect and authority in the workplace. Sometimes women need to make a strict fashion statement and when they do, they look more powerful with boots on.

The American general George Patton said: 'A soldier in shoes is only a soldier; but in boots he becomes a warrior.' Patton understood that boots are symbolic of power – and this is the case whether worn in battle or in the boardroom. When former United States Secretary of State Condaleezza Rice inspected the troops in 2005 she wore knee-high boots with her civilian clothing: at Wiesbaden, a US military base in Germany, she chose an ensemble that projected machismo, power and strength. Her overcoat was minimal and militaristic, and her stiletto-heeled boots were black, sculpted close to the calf and undeniably feminine. Rice's image was striking because she looked tough and authoritarian, yet her boots' high heels and shapely uppers gave her ensemble a feminine air. By shedding the matronliness of Madeleine Albright and the neutrality of Hillary Clinton, she set a new image standard for political women.

The relationship between the body and fashion has changed dramatically in recent years. Women seek to achieve strong, attractive bodies that are at least partially exposed by modern clothing, yet they want to feel protected at the same time. Just as modern fashion is polarized around extremes such as hard and soft, inside and outside, flexible and firm, so contemporary women combine opposites to create looks that make them feel empowered. Feminine styles are intimate and seductive, while boots temper them with protectiveness and power. As women step forward in looks like these, they channel the ghosts of history's transgressive warrior women.

WEAPONS FOR WOMEN

Joan of Arc may be an unlikely fashion icon, but she was the first woman in Europe to don military boots. She wore thigh-high cuissardes when she rode into battle, and she won victories more swiftly than any man had done. Because Joan was wearing boots and armour when she was captured, the English threw her into a military prison rather than locking her up at the convent where female prisoners of war were held. At her trial in 1431, one of the charges brought against her was that she had worn men's boots both on and off the battlefield, and this was the only 'crime' of which she said she was guilty.

Opposite:
Joan of Arc wore metal-plated cuissardes when she rode into battle, and is said to have worn thigh-high boots even off the battlefield. Her feminine strength and androgynous style would later inspire the fashion and footwear collections of many top designers.

Yet it seems that armed women have always had boots on. A marble relief on display at the British Museum depicts two female gladiators. Each has an adopted *nom de guerre* and is armed with a sword and shield, ankle boots and heavy greaves (shin protectors). The practice of female combat was established during Nero's rule (AD 54–68) and banned by Septimius Severus around AD 200. The gladiatrix's boots were both weapon and armour; the gladiatrix could wound her opponent with a karate-like kick and shield herself with her soles if thrown on to her back.

Although gladiatrices no longer exist, the boots they appropriated from their male counterparts still do. Thanks to a wave of gladiator chic that swept through the footwear collections of 2007 and 2008, the gladiator boot came back into fashion as a sexy open-toe staple for the modern wardrobe. Designers pushed bootwear to the limits by reinventing conventional uppers as web-like shafts or strong leather nets. The boots were crafted with platform soles, wedge heels, flat soles or pointed stilettos, and were secured to the wearer's feet with leather strips or wide laces. They looked too elegant to be worn in combat, but they were certainly chic enough to wield unmistakable style.

Designers such as Versace, Chanel, Balmain and Dolce & Gabbana stayed true to traditional gladiator styles, designing boots that had flat soles and lateral straps, and typically used wide bands of leather on the front and back of the leg to support the upper. One of Dolce & Gabbana's gladiator styles was a simple bootie fashioned from just eight colourful straps. Each piece was made from a different kind of leather or snakeskin, giving the boots a variety of rich textures and tones.

Azzedine Alaïa's elegant designs also remained faithful to the gladiator boot's original style. Flat-soled, sandal-like vamps were trimmed in python leather that snaked around the feet and formed a shaft between the ankle and the knee. The laces trailed around to the back of the boot and tied just under the knee. Alaïa created an ankle-boot model crafted from criss-cross leather straps that looked as if the boots had been woven on the wearer's feet.

Balenciaga designed several styles of gladiator boots for the Autumn/ Winter 2008 collection. One style defied traditional footwear, being assembled piece by piece from hundreds of leather components rather than cut out of hide and sewn together. Another one of Balenciaga's knee-high styles resembled a corset more than footwear. The boots laced up from their open toes to the knee, mimicking the intricate craftsmanship of a Victorian corset.

Alexander McQueen's version of the gladiator boot lashed the foot on to a stiletto heel and encased the shin in delicate serpentine shapes sculpted from soft leather. As the boot laced up the back of the leg, its leather laces became an integral part of the overall design.

For their Spring/Summer 2007 collection, Givenchy created flesh-toned boots with soft, open-toed vamps and uppers comprised of leather bands criss-crossing randomly around the lower leg. They also launched several open-toe ankle styles with streamlined soles, stiletto heels and thick leather bands to secure them to the ankle. Their gladiator-style bootie was made in metal-coloured leather, adding an industrial edge to its fierce silhouette.

Sergio Rossi's 'Chains' gladiator boot encased the foot in a series of hoops that recalled the flexible frame of an old-fashioned crinoline, while their painted python gladiator bootie was crafted from chain-like leather links that lay flat across the bridge of the foot and the ankle. Etro took a unique approach by introducing an ethnic element to the gladiator style, trimming the front of the boot with rows of leather fringe to add a note of Native American design.

Dior reminded women what gladiator boots are for: kicking. Unlike the open-toe styles favoured by most designers, Dior's gladiator booties were made with bands of thick leather that criss-crossed over the toe and provided protection for the feet. Crafted with hefty platform soles that would add extra momentum if the wearer swung her foot, the boot would create lasting damage with just one mighty kick.

SUPERHEROES OF STYLE

Since the first appearance of comic-book legend Superman in 1938, designers across the world have been fascinated by superheroes. Superman and a host of similar heroes are icons of physical strength and supernatural power. They have an unmistakable style: they dress meticulously in unitards and close-fitting garments, drape capes romantically around their shoulders and stand tall in high boots. Like Superman, whose emblem was one of the first logos to be embroidered on clothing, they brandish a crest of honour and deploy an armoury of special weapons and crime-busting gadgetry.

Ordinary women may not be armed with a superhero's arsenal, but they can accessorize themselves with weapon-like objects. Heavy chains are disguised as belts and straps, and massive knuckleduster rings promise to pack a mighty punch. A pair of stiletto-heeled boots can function as a pair of spikes sharp enough to wound any man unlucky enough to fall beneath them. At times, the fashioned body even seems to model itself on the superhero's physique; by using shoulder pads, corsets, push-up bras and even surgical implants, women are shaped into the superhero's idealized form.

Although fashion idolizes the style of the superheroes, it is even more in awe of their ability to metamorphose from ordinary human beings to creatures with special powers. All superheroes assume the guise of ordinary men and women; once they rip off their street clothes and unfurl their capes, the change of dress magically transforms them – an ability women everywhere would love to have. Although clothing alone can't endow them with supernatural powers, fashion provides a plethora of opportunities to reshape the body and remake the self, giving women scope to empower themselves in heroic style.

A new type of fashionable woman started to evolve during the 1990s. Whereas historically women were portrayed with exaggerated sexual characteristics that made them passive objects, designers started equipping them with the means to take charge. Jean Paul Gaultier famously launched his 'Femmes Amazone' collection for Autumn/Winter 1995, presenting cybernetic seductresses equipped with the technological means of outsmarting their suitors. Shown the same season, Thierry Mugler's collection included women encased in robot-like suits of cyber-style armour, conjuring visions of a cyborg queen more than a flesh-and-blood creature. He had previously shown super-hero-like armour in 1991, which appeared to contain weapon-like gadgets. These cyborgian looks, whether worn with boots or not, transformed women into strong, complex characters with heightened abilities.

For his Spring/Summer 2005 collection, Alexander McQueen created images of superhero-like women and equipped them to use brute force if necessary. McQueen's heroines were kitted out in American football sports equipment. Hard helmets and professional shoulder pads were worn with thigh-high boots, hot pants and halters, conveying an image of sexuality and power. Two years later, Balenciaga's Spring/Summer 2007 collection included women encased in surfaces made from hard leather and cool metal. They wore leggings made from metal pieces and gladiator-like footwear constructed from industrial components. The look evoked an image of fashion's future, yet also recalled the sandals and greaves worn by gladiatrices in the ancient world.

Opposite, left:
Alexander McQueen's Spring/Summer 2005 collection featured women wearing the clothing of attack. While the models' upper bodies were padded and protected, their footwear was feminine and demure.

Opposite, right:
Emma Peel (played by Diana Rigg) was one of the first 'warrior women' to be featured in a television series, the 1960s *The Avengers*. Sexy and strong, Mrs Peel characteristically wore high leather boots.

Direct references to superheroes abound in contemporary fashion. Strong, smart and sexy, Wonder Woman has been on the fashion radar since she was brought to life in the American television series starring Lynda Carter in the 1970s. Wonder Woman had previously featured as one of the principal superheroes of DC Comics and the first female superhero – she was feminine, sported an enviable cinched waist and flaunted bare skin. During the Second World War and the postwar era, she was a patriotic hero on a mission to defend America, and sported red, white and blue costumes that were composites of the American flag. Her boots were handmade from supple red leather and trimmed with wide white bands at the top. The zips running down the inside seam, along with the rest of the detailing, were impeccably stitched.

Designers such as John Galliano, Bernard Wilhelm and Viktor & Rolf understood that every woman would like to look and behave like Wonder Woman. Lynda Carter's portrayal made Wonder Woman something of an American icon, as she stood with hands on hips, raven hair billowing over her shoulders and shimmering red boots planted firmly on the ground. Possibly inspired more by the actress than by the character herself, Viktor & Rolf gave Wonder Woman a chic makeover in their Autumn/Winter 2000 collection, dressing her in a long jacket, chic ruffled tunic, smart trousers and boots. Every item in the ensemble was covered in the characteristic stars and stripes of Wonder Woman's costume, suggesting that superhero chic was now in vogue.

Bernard Wilhelm's Spring/Summer 2008 collection included star-spangled tops and hot pants. With their red-and-blue stripes and white stars they seemed to be a costume for Wonder Women's hip teenage daughter. Wilhelm paired the ensembles with platform-soled, silver-coloured leather boots that added a strong retro element. Footwear designers have paid homage to Wonder Woman too – Ellie's 'Liberty' boot proposed an alternative to her red knee boots. Their PVC boots feature the red, white and blue of the American flag, taking Wonder Woman back to her patriotic roots.

PUSS IN BOOTS

Superhero Catwoman is a seductive feline beauty. She first appeared in the 'Batman No. 1' comic in 1940, and was simply referred to as The Cat, a female burglar. Originally the character was a hedonistic socialite whose compulsion to steal stemmed from ennui. Over the years, her character and her costume

Opposite:
Like that of Superman, Wonder Woman's uniform was carefully designed. Her red, white and blue colourways attested to her American patriotism, while her boots suggested her resilience and strength.

Below:
Michelle Pfeiffer played Catwoman in the film *Batman Returns* (1992) using playfully feline gestures to convey a lethal combination of sex appeal and violence. Her shiny patent leather thigh-high boots were modelled on the type a dominatrix would wear.

have been reinvented several times. Today, she generally sports the PVC catsuit worn by Michelle Pfeiffer in 1992 film *Batman Returns*. In the film, Catwoman made this herself out of a shiny black raincoat, borrowing parts of her sewing kit to make the claws. Accessorized with a whip, gloves and knee-high, high-heeled platform boots, the costume is strongly reminiscent of dominatrix style, lending an air of fetishistic sexuality to the character. Michelle Pfeiffer reinforced Catwoman's dominatrix disposition by alternating between lioness-like alpha-cat behaviour and kittenish flirtation. She brandished her whip like a lady lion-tamer, expertly cracking it to keep others at bay.

Catwoman's influence among designers has been strong, especially in the works of Gianni Versace, Thierry Mugler, John Galliano, Alexander McQueen and Jean Paul Gaultier. These designers have a long-held fascination with fetishistic clothing and footwear, and were among the first to present garments made in shiny materials such as patent leather, rubber and PVC on the catwalks. One of the most memorable expressions of Catwoman was created by Thierry Mugler for his Autumn/Winter 1996 collection. Mugler designed a form-fitting black leather trouser suit and polished it to a high sheen. Complete with a cape, mask and thigh-high boots, Mugler reclaimed Catwoman as a couture classic.

Batwoman, like Catwoman, was a sexy superhero who appeared in the Batman series. The original Batwoman emerged in 1956 and was killed off in 1979. She was reborn in 2006 as a tall superhero with flowing red hair, knee-high red boots with spiked 13-centimetre (five-inch) heels, and a form-fitting black outfit. Out of costume, the new Batwoman shares the same name as her original human character, Kathy Kane. Like Catwoman, Batwoman is a socialite from Gotham City high society by day and assumes an alter ego by night to wage war against the villains of the world. When Batwoman was reborn, her mask and hair were changed to soften her look, and the yellow accents on the black costume were changed to deep scarlet. The costume's dark colour and strict design belie the character's nocturnal manoeuvres. Not only is black associated with fear, death and the supernatural, it also connotes surprise, stealth and concealment.

Any woman can claim to have superhero style with the right boots on. Boot styles that reproduce the symbols and insignias of a superhero often generate cult followings. Male heroes such as Superman, Batman, Spiderman and The Flash have all had their emblems appliquéd on women's boots, and the curved nails of Catwoman's paws have been etched on leather booties. Women with flames licking at the edge of their boots may be paying homage to PyroMan as they hotfoot it around the city. Spiderman's web has formed a motif on several boot models, as have Wonder Woman's stars and stripes. A woman wearing superhero footwear may not necessarily set out to save the world, but her boots are likely to conquer the men swooning at her feet.

GIVENCHY

The house of Givenchy was founded in 1952 by designer Hubert de Givenchy, who based the brand on understated, elegant styles that muted the extravagant silhouettes created by rival designer Christian Dior. Givenchy's clients were regarded as socially confident but also as sartorially discreet. Audrey Hepburn, Princess Grace and Jackie Kennedy famously wore Givenchy, associating the brand with good taste more than cutting-edge style. Hubert de Givenchy's retirement in 1995 led to an unsettled period, with four creative directors following one another in quick succession; since 2005 the young Italian designer Riccardo Tisci has been head of womenswear and haute couture. Tisci's penchant for Gothic glamour and futuristic minimalism has created a new type of Givenchy woman, and the boots she wears are edgy and empowering.

Givenchy introduced a new type of boot in the Autumn/Winter 2008 collection, known as the 'gaiter' style. Sometimes called spats, the boots have an extended cuff that falls all the way from the knee to the instep. The cuffs add a touch of *trompe l'oeil* trickery that creates the illusion of a leather trouser-leg concealing the boot beneath. The style is robust yet stylish, masculine yet elegant, giving women a strong stance that still appears feminine and chic.

When a group of women were interviewed by the author as to which boots would make them feel most like a warrioress, many of them claimed that a pair of Givenchy's tall slouch boots would be the perfect choice. The boots are robust in style, are made from distressed leather, and are fitted with rodeo-style rope details and a drawstring top. The women liked the fact that the distressed leather looked dirty, which gave these boots a tougher image. Although fans of Givenchy may not need to look like a superhero or a gladiatrice to feel powerful, they still regard style as an important weapon.

ABOVE: These peep-toe ankle boots from Givenchy's Autumn/Winter 2007 collection were made in soft leather that enveloped the entire upper and heel in a textured surface.

OPPOSITE: With their pointed toes, wedge heels and streamlined uppers, these boots from Autumn/Winter 2008 appear almost aerodynamic in design.

OVERLEAF: Each season Givenchy brings out striking new styles that are both sexy and sophisticated. Peep-toe designs featured in the Autumn/Winter 2008 collection (far left), while these pointy toe, thigh-high boots with rows of metal studs down the back were the highlight of Autumn/Winter 2007 (left). Chic animal prints reigned in Autumn/Winter 1997 (right), while gladiator boots set the tone for the Spring/Summer 2008 collection (far right).

ALEXANDER MCQUEEN

Fashion has always been a cruel mistress, and in the world of Alexander McQueen, it still is. Perhaps no other brand illustrates this point so perfectly as McQueen. Models have been shackled in leg irons and their faces distorted with mouth and eye jewellery; they have been dressed up in tightly laced corsets and made to walk in crippling heels. Yet its followers claim that the controversial garments and strictly tailored boots are worth wearing at any price, and that McQueen's footwear is actually more comfortable than most.

From the first collection, the McQueen woman has always been a warrior, armed with weapons of jewellery and accessories that equip her with the means of aggression or self-defence. Feminine beauty is often portrayed in terms of aggression and brutality, assigning women the ability to wound and attack. The boots are typically made with spiky wingtips that could cause considerable damage if wielded in a kick. Pointed stiletto heels appear razor-sharp, so sleek they seem to balance the wearer's foot atop the tip of a sabre's blade.

McQueen is known for visionary designs, but when it comes to footwear the biggest challenge was making a pair of prosthetic legs. Paralympic sprinter Aimee Mullins was invited to model in the catwalk presentation of the '#13' collection (Spring/Summer 1999), with the promise that she would be provided with artificial legs to blend in with the collection. The prosthetic legs resembled boots that rose to the knee, carved in wood and styled exactly like the other footwear shown that season. Good boots are often likened to being an extension of the feet and legs; in designing prosthetics, McQueen mastered the ultimate challenge that a footwear designer can face.

OPPOSITE: The sparkling gems on these jewel-encrusted boots from Spring/Summer 2009 were meticulously fitted together like the pieces of a jigsaw puzzle.

ABOVE LEFT: From the Autumn/Winter 2003 collection, these crimson-coloured boots make a strong statement when paired with a black-and-white garment against a black-and-white background.

ABOVE RIGHT: Three leather tongues appear to overlap in this boot design for the Autumn/Winter 2008 collection.

OVERLEAF, LEFT: From the drawing board to design and production of the final product, attention to detail makes McQueen's boots a combination of exquisite style, innovation and art.

OVERLEAF, RIGHT, TOP AND BOTTOM: McQueen's boots are often a perfect balance of tradition and technical innovation. The buttons and buckles used in these boots' design suggest Victorian influences, while their construction is underpinned by state-of-the-art technology.

8
FUTURE STRIDES

FRESH DIRECTIONS

The future directions of footwear are not set in stone, but offer rather an entire spectrum of possibilities to exploit. All of fashion is moving forward by forging new alliances with technology, architecture and design, and the boot is no exception. The young, upcoming designers of today are radically reinventing its relationship to the body and to the built environment. And as footwear design becomes increasingly underpinned by principles of sustainability, the new boot styles that result are pioneering fresh directions for the entire industry.

As today's generation of designers breaks fresh ground, many are working in response to new developments in digital technology and material science. Dynamic and interactive materials have the power to change how footwear is both manufactured and experienced. The elements of our world are becoming stronger, faster, lighter and smarter; unbreakable gossamer fibres can heave a satellite into orbit, yet are soft enough to be worn on the foot. Super-strong materials are able to incorporate technology, and many of them integrate software, communication devices and information exchanges. High-performance substrates are synthesized to make these materials both flexible and wearable, resulting in boots with eye-catching optical effects and tactile textures.

While the new generation of boots promises to be high-tech, some established designers have voiced their resolve to remain true to time-honoured traditions and classic materials. Many of footwear's rising stars are working with a wide range of components, creating styles that align craftsmanship with both sustainable elements and high-tech processes. As these designers transform the materials of the past into fresh inspirations for the present, their works are signposting new directions for the boots of tomorrow.

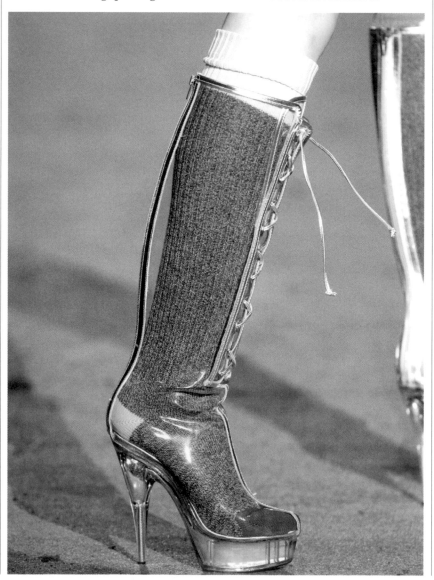

Left:
Canadian fashion brand D Squared produce some of the edgiest boots around. These platform boots from the Spring/Summer 2010 collection feature a see-through sole and transparent upper.

Opposite:
When Antonio Berardi presented heel-less boots in the Autumn/Winter 2008 collection, critics marvelled at this genuinely innovative style. Although it looks as if it would be impossible to walk in them, women who have tried them claim that they move like any other high-heeled boot.

TECHNO BOOTS

Wearable technology promises to transform fashion and footwear. By embedding mobile communication networks into the clothing we wear, our garments will be able to exchange signals with remote systems. An energy source is needed to power such devices, and researchers are investigating ways of harnessing the kinetic energy generated by the body as it moves. Boots, more than shoes, are ideal for storing the energy generated by the wearer's strides from as simple an activity as walking around town. Because boots are generally bulkier than shoes, the required circuitry, power cells and transceivers will be more easily concealed in them.

As a mobile power source, boots would be central to the creation and consumption of wearable technologies. Not only will future boots be able to engage with remote systems, they will even establish networks that can be brought under the wearer's control. Imagine being able to activate overhead lights with a click of the heel, or dial a number by wiggling a big toe. Wearers wouldn't flinch if calls were terminated unexpectedly, but merely outline a small circle with the left heel to redial, or stomp the right foot twice to hang up.

Just as interactive technology and digital media hold the potential to re-equip the boot radically, so they also provide the tools for transforming its appearance. The boots of the future will be made from pliable synthetic skins incorporating interactive digital networks and sensors that glean information from, and trigger reactions to, the wearer's surroundings, including light, heat and pressure. Gel cavities will expand and contract according to the wearer's gait, ensuring maximum comfort at all times. As technology takes it into the future, the boot promises to maximize the body's potential as it creates new frontiers for wearable technology.

FUTURISTIC SILHOUETTES

The laws of physiology and human proportion dictate that a boot should be constructed according to certain rules. Today, visionary designers are thinking beyond all limitations, creating boots that are independent of pre-existing ideas about form and look. As they introduce radical new designs, the only rule they seem to follow is that the boot should somehow accommodate the human foot. The designers pioneering these innovations imitate the skills of an architect or an engineer more than those of a traditional bootmaker. Some of the avant-garde designs emerging demonstrate a new understanding of mass as well as space, featuring lightweight metals, reinforced plastics, glass fibres and industrial mesh, crafted in cutting-edge designs. Their streamlined shapes and resilient surfaces are often more characteristic of contemporary architecture than of conventional footwear.

As a form, boots are one of the most interesting within the fashion industry. Their structure enables them to stand upright even when independent of the body. Like architectural edifices, boots are three-dimensional objects with volume and mass; their interior is hollow, recalling the volume of space that lies within a building's outer walls. The heel and the sole provide a foundation for the rest of the boot, anchoring the upper to the shank as an architect would angle a building over a slope. Footwear brand Espace have applied an architectural technique to boot design, creating a breathtakingly contemporary style. Espace designed a metal support that combines the heel and sole in a single expression. It has the effect of cantilevering the vamp from the heel, which introduces an architectural device to boot design.

Boots are also becoming more aerodynamic in appearance. Mirroring the sleek new styles in the automotive and aerospace industries, boots with tapered shapes are starting to gain ground. Their aerodynamic appearances look as though they are intended to amplify the body's capacity for speed. They weigh less than conventional styles, enabling the wearer to move more rapidly than they could in heavy boots. Brazilian fashion designer Alexandre Herchcovitch has created a signature boot so streamlined that it takes minimalism to a higher level. Likened to a sci-fi design, its tapered vamp and wedge sole seem to be heralding a future trend.

Opposite:
Fashion designer Alexandre Herchcovitch creates boots that get noticed. Herchcovitch's Autumn/Winter 2008 collection featured boots designed with new digital media and crafted in cutting-edge materials.

Overleaf, left:
United Nudes explore a wide range of design techniques. Their Möbius boot is crafted with a sole reminiscent of a mathematical Möbius strip, a twisting plane that has only one surface.

Overleaf, right:
For the Spring/Summer 2010 collection, Rick Owens created futuristic silhouettes based on asymmetrical shapes, pointed collars and otherworldly outlines. The mood of the collection was captured in these slouch-style, peep-toe boots, which suggest that boots are moving away from form-fitting, streamlined styles.

Designers are exploring the extent to which boots can be constructed as geometric objects. Boots designed using computer software employ mathematical equations to calculate lengths, angles, areas and volumes, making it easy to map out prism-like shapes and cubist-inspired surfaces. Such boots are designed in terms of points, lines and planes as much as fashion and fit.

Heels are also moving away from traditional shapes and morphing into geometric forms: cones, inverted pyramids, cylinders and spheres often feature in new styles. Uppers are spiralling around the leg like a Möbius strip, the single continuous curve that forms a wide, contouring band. Other shapes are so curvilinear that they appear to have been designed with a compass rather than with traditional instruments.

In recent years Balenciaga have gained a reputation as one of the biggest innovators in footwear. Balenciaga's boots are designed with curves so complex and angles so radical that they resemble sculptural abstractions more than footwear. By using a combination of soft leather and moulded rubber, Balenciaga's designers have created fractals and folds that make richly textured surfaces. Alexander McQueen's luxurious jet crystal boot has one of the most stunningly geometric surfaces ever seen in footwear. The facets of the cut stones create a shimmering prismatic sheath that cascades over the entire boot.

Contrasting sharply with strict geometric styles, boots that explore new volumes around the foot have also come into fashion. These styles banish the tyranny of traditional styling, sometimes creating formless, abstract shapes that decentre conventional perspectives and undermine any single viewpoint. Yves Saint Laurent is taking boot shapes to new spatial extremes, resulting in a range of striking silhouettes. One of the most innovative is an ankle boot that is commonly described as 'hoof-like'. The boot is comprised of a platform sole, a wedge heel and an upper that rises to the ankle. All parts of the boot are covered in a seamless leather piece, as if the entire design was carved out of a solid object.

The London-based Italian fashion designer Antonio Berardi is pioneering a daring new type of footwear that eliminates the need for a heel. Berardi's gravity-defying heel-less boots may look as if they are impossible to walk in, but, according to the designer, they feel just like any other pair of 13-centimetre (five-inch) heels. The boots' platform sole is much wider than most high heels, providing ample support for the foot. Although heel-less boots may hold the foot sufficiently, medical experts warn that such footwear may alter a wearer's stride. Worn consistently over time, there is a risk that they could change the natural gait.

Above:
The Autumn/Winter 2008 collections featured fresh silhouettes and new materials. The theme of transparency emerged in several guises, showcasing the toes yet making the heel of the boot 'invisible'. Noticeably, boot uppers began creeping down the leg, almost meeting shoe proportions, as seen in this design by Ferragamo.

Opposite, left:
Thigh-high boots are among the oldest styles, created to protect and insulate the feet and legs. For Autumn/Winter 2009, Alexandre Herchcovitch combined a traditional style with an edgy heel.

Opposite, top right:
Yves Saint Laurent pared down the boot to the bare essentials for Autumn/Winter 2008. A slender stiletto heel meets a minimalistic upper, bringing simplified styling to the height of footwear fashion.

Opposite, bottom right:
Balenciaga stepped out of the conventional footwear mould to design boots in bold geometric shapes. The Autumn/Winter 2008 collection presented boots like these that seemed to redefine the shape of the feet.

SHREDDED CHIC

At the beginning of the 1990s, radical fashion designers pioneered a look characterized by visible stitching, reversed seams, raw edges, exposed linings and loose threads. Their work mirrored a style of architecture in which a building's structure was unveiled and its construction elements made visible. Just as architects may choose to reveal pipes, ducts, shafts and cables, fashion designers may opt to expose elements of tailoring traditionally hidden from view. The deconstructivist style was initially viewed as an anti-fashion movement that challenged the prevailing notions of clothing design. The aesthetic that resulted reverses the process of clothing construction by introducing a method almost antithetical to couture techniques.

Around 2000, deconstruction began to influence footwear, spreading over from the shredded chic of fashion. Boots made with transparent platform soles enabled hardware to be seen, showcasing the fixtures and fittings that hold the vamp in place. The crystal-like heel of Dior's mesh bootie reveals the screws that fix it to the sole. The leather and metal vamp resembles chain mail, bringing the entire foot into view though still anchoring it firmly to the sole.

Deconstructivist architects will often cut away sections of a building's façade, replacing them with glass to break up its mass and make its inner parts visible from the outside. A similar trend emerged in boots when the Autumn/ Winter collections of 2008 and 2009 presented a multitude of cut-away styles. Such designers as Dior, Loeffler Randall, Cesare Paciotti and Chloé crafted boots from wide leather bands with open spaces in between that made the wearer's flesh visible. Ungaro took the style to an extreme in an elegant knee-high design, while Givenchy created an abstract style in which panels of leather seemed to have been randomly cut away. Christian Louboutin and Dior used panels of pliable mesh that broke down the boot's mass and created one of the season's most eye-catching designs.

ULTRA MATERIALS

Future boot styles may reflect innovation in materials more than in fashion trends. Historically, the use of extreme materials has occurred more in fashion than in footwear, but that has begun to change in recent years. Sports shoes were the first form of footwear to explore the materials and technologies used elsewhere in design. The sports industry has always taken the lead in progressing high-performance footwear technology, and many of the new materials it uses are as suited to boot designs as they are to trainers.

Opposite:
Viktor & Rolf's vertiginous padded platform boots encase the leg in a style that brought surgical brace supports to mind. They follow the trend for effacing the heel, and create a fresh silhouette for knee boots.

Right:
The Venice-based Stephen footwear brand is renowned for designing boots with bold new shapes and silhouettes. This streamlined version of a slouch boot cocoons the leg in comfort as well as style.

One such material is aerogel, an inorganic, lightweight, solid-state substance derived from gel in which liquid has been replaced with gas. Among its innumerable uses, aerogel has remarkable potential as a boot material. It weighs virtually nothing yet can support a great amount of weight. It can be manufactured in thin sheets, beads, panels and moulded parts, and made transparent, translucent or opaque. Material scientists consider aerogel to be the best insulation material ever invented. It has unsurpassed thermal insulation values, as well as being a superb sound and shock absorber. Adapted for boot design, the material could be used to create styles moulded from a single aerogel piece. Other applications include creating an aerogel web that would create suspension for the foot to position it more comfortably inside the boot.

Liquid plastics promise to shape the boots of the future, according to Freedom of Creation, an Amsterdam-based research lab that advances rapid prototyping processes for product design. Freedom of Creation discovered that rapid prototyping – a process that produces objects by building up thin layers of plastic that harden as they dry – could create forms that would be impossible to produce by traditional manufacturing processes such as moulding or pressing. Freedom of Creation have employed the technique to create objects including garments, accessories, shoes and boots, proving that rapid prototyping processes could be used to make the boots of the future.

Future boot-wearers may never have to clean their boots and soles, thanks to developments within biomimicry, a relatively new science that finds ways to imitate natural phenomena. Researchers have been inspired by the lotus leaf's ability to remain clean in muddy environments. It emerges from the earth without a speck of dirt on it due to its unique surface texture. The lotus flower forces water to form droplets and roll away rather than slide off. As they do so, the droplets pick up dirt, mud or small insects in their way, just as a snowball accumulates mass as it tumbles down a hill. Applied to a boot, such a surface could virtually wash itself, or wipe clean with just a squirt of water.

It may be possible for the rest of the boot to mimic a natural organism too. Dutch designer Bart Hess believes that the barriers between nature and technology can be broken down. Hess's conceptual boot expresses a vision of a design that is partly robotic, partly organic, and pulses with hidden intelligence that enables the boots to communicate with each other. Hess's boots themselves have 'legs', enabling them to assist the wearer when she walks, or provide extra traction to keep her from slipping down an incline.

Fashionistas looking for sustainable style are likely to buy their boots from Stella McCartney, the London-based designer who kicked off the trend for eco-conscious footwear several seasons ago. McCartney is pioneering a model of leather-free 'vegan' footwear, made without any harm to animals. Her ethical message is one of the strongest in high-end fashion and footwear, and provides a sought-after alternative in an industry based on animal hides. As McCartney, and practitioners like her, dare to look beyond traditional materials, they update the styles of the past with fresh visions for the footwear to come. Future boots can do more than just keep women a step ahead of fashion, they may even keep the rest of the industry on its toes.

Above left:
Stella McCartney is a pioneer when it comes to ethical footwear. Her boot designs are environmentally friendly, yet striking and chic.

Above right:
Marni's commitment to natural materials often adds a strong elemental signature to their footwear designs. These boots are crafted with wooden platforms and heels which provide a potent contrast to the soft, supple leather uppers.

Opposite:
United Nudes combine style with efficiency in this boot design, which provides pockets for money, gadgets and mobile phones. The style suggests combat boots, as if equipping the wearer for conflict.

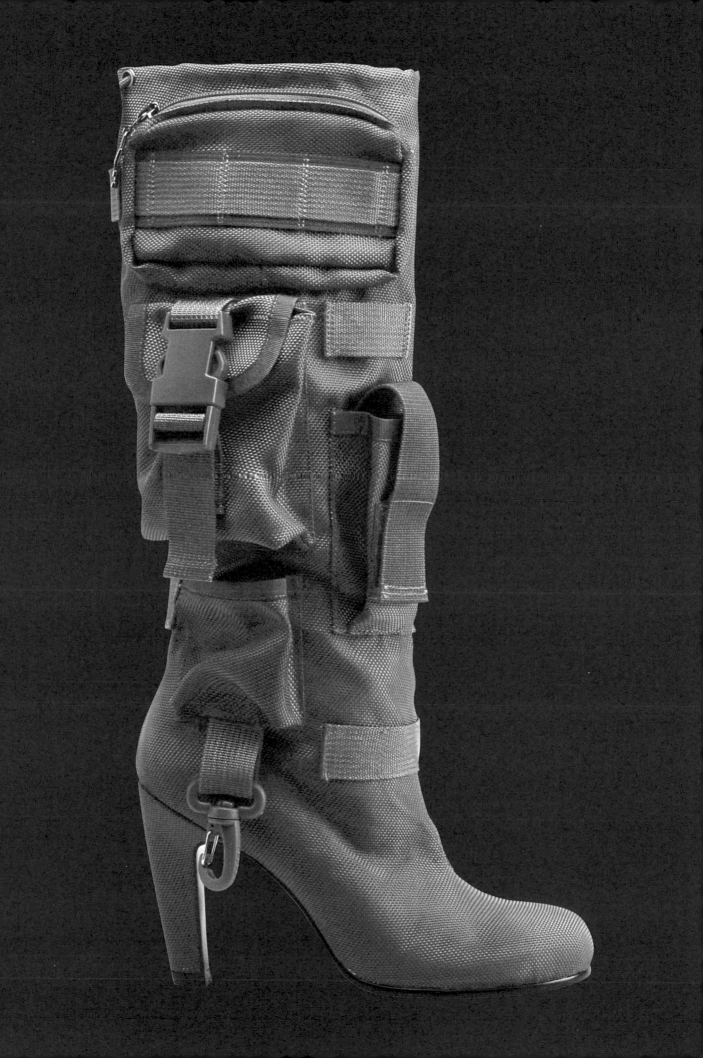

A.F. VANDEVORST

Belgian designers An Vandevorst and Filip Arickx met while studying at the Royal Academy of Fine Arts in Antwerp. A married couple, they set up the A.F. Vandevorst label after graduation, and showed their first fashion collection in Paris in 1997. From their studio in Antwerp, they produce a complete women's ready-to-wear line that includes garments, handbags, accessories and lingerie. Their footwear is developed and manufactured in Italy.

A.F. Vandevorst describe themselves as 'a company in full expansion with a keen eye for the future'. Since launching their footwear collection, they have produced a range of chic boots crafted in traditional silhouettes that introduce a new dynamic to boot design. Ankle boots, knee boots and equestrian styles are typically fitted with high heels made from wood or textured leather, embellished with stitched detailing and crafted with rounded toes. Drawing on their expertise in ruching and in draping fabric, A.F. Vandevorst mould calfskin to the wearer's feet and legs as if creating a second skin.

Felt has a long history as a traditional bootmaking material, and A.F. Vandevorst gave the fabric a futuristic twist in their striking felt-and-leather 'Horse Hoof' designs. The style is made in several versions, with heights ranging from the ankle to the thigh. The boot's platform sole is hidden beneath a broad band of leather that mimics the shape of a horse's hoof, giving the traditional boot shape an unexpected equine outline. As the brand continues to experiment with unconventional materials and to design visionary new shapes, A.F. Vandevorst are a boot line to watch.

RIGHT: The 'horse hoof' boot was one of the most eye-catching footwear designs launched in the Autumn/Winter 2009 collections. Described by the press as 'equine', the felt and leather boots' stiletto heels were higher than others in the collection, causing some models to wobble down the catwalk like newborn foals.

OVERLEAF, LEFT: A.F. Vandevorst created a palette of earth tones for their Spring/Summer 2010 collection, colouring garments and footwear in beige, fawn and taupe.

OVERLEAF, RIGHT: The designers typically include both classical boots and visionary designs in their footwear collections, indicating that classic styles, such as these riding boots, are likely to be as popular in the future as they have been for the past three decades.

INDEX

Page numbers in *italic* refer to captions

PICTURE CREDITS

Cover and chapter openers:
Lovisa Burfitt, www.agentsandartists.com

6	© Hulton-Deutsch Collection / CORBIS
8	Image courtesy of The Shoe Collection, Northampton Museums
9	© Douglas Kirkland / CORBIS
13	The Art Archive / Archaeological Museum, Istanbul / Gianni Dagli Orti
14	The Art Archive / Museo Civico Cristiano, Brescia / Gianni Dagli Orti
15	Hulton Archive / Getty Images
17	The Art Archive / Chandler-Pohrt Collection / Buffalo Bill Historical Center, Cody, Wyoming / NA.202.469
18	The Art Archive / Real Biblioteca de el Escorial / Gianni Dagli Orti
19	Private Collection / The Bridgeman Art Library
20	The Art Archive / Bibliothèque Municipale Rouen / Gianni Dagli Orti
22l	The Art Archive / Kharbine-Tapabor
22r	The Art Archive / Culver Pictures
23	Courtesy of the BATA Shoe Museum
24	KRAKSTROM / Rex Features
25	John Kobal Foundation / Getty Images
26	Keystone / Getty Images
27tl	© John French / V&A Images / Victoria & Albert Museum
27tr	© Bettmann / CORBIS
27b	Harry Dempster / Express / Getty Images
28, 29	© Anthea Simms
30	Courtesy of Sergio Rossi. Photographer Jenny Van Sommers
31	© Photo B.D.V. / CORBIS
32–35	Courtesy of Joseph Azagury
39	Dove / Express / Getty Images
40	Photofest / Retna
42	Catwalking.com
43	Courtesy John Galliano
44	Benhamou & Valente / Liaison / Getty Images
46	Catwalking.com
47l	© Anthea Simms
47r	© Stardust Fashion
48	© Anthea Simms
49	© Cardinale Stephane / CORBIS SYGMA
50	Courtesy Cesare Paciotti
51–52, 53bl, 54–55	Catwalking.com
53tl, 53tr, 53br	Courtesy Chanel
56	Courtesy Christian Dior
57tl, 57tr	Catwalking.com
57bl	© Anthea Simms
57br	Catwalking.com
58–59	Courtesy Christian Dior
62	© Donald Graham / CORBIS
63	© Lynn Goldsmith / CORBIS
64l	Catwalking.com
64tr, 64br	© Anthea Simms
65	Image courtesy of The Shoe Collection, Northampton Museums
66, 67l	Catwalking.com
67r	© Anthea Simms
68	© Steven Cook
69	Photo by Dave Hogan / Getty Images
70–71	Ellen Von Unwerth, Casadei 50th Anniversary ©
72	Courtesy of Ellie Shoes
74l	F/W09–10 sketch by Francesco Russo, Creative Director of Sergio Rossi. Courtesy Sergio Rossi
74m, 74r	Courtesy Sergio Rossi
75	Courtesy Sergio Rossi – Photography by David Slijper. Modelled by Anouk Lepere of IMG models.
76	Miles Aldridge / trunkarchive.com
77	Courtesy Sergio Rossi
78–81	Images by Ilaria Orsini for Casadei 50th Anniversary
85	Courtesy Muks
86	© Anthea Simms
89	Courtesy Edoche
90	Courtesy John Galliano
93tl	© Anthea Simms
93tr	Catwalking.com
93b	Pedro Ugarte / AFP / Getty Images
94	Catwalking.com
95	© Roger De La Harpe, Gallo Images / CORBIS
96–97	Courtesy Manolo Blahnik Archive
98	© Wayne Tippetts
99	Catwalking.com
100–101	Courtesy Viktor & Rolf
102l, 102tr	© Anthea Simms
102br	Courtesy Viktor & Rolf
103	© Anthea Simms
106l	Catwalking.com
106r	© Anthea Simms
107	© Steven Cook
108–109	Catwalking.com
110l	© Anthea Simms
110r	Catwalking.com
111	Image courtesy of The Shoe Collection, Northampton Museums
112⊠113	© Neal Preston / CORBIS
114–115	Catwalking.com
117	Courtesy Tamara Henriques
118tl	© Anthea Simms
118tr, 118bl, 118br	Catwalking.com
119l	© Anthea Simms
119r	Photo by Time Life Pictures / DMI / Getty Images
120–121	Courtesy Marc Jacobs
122, 123l	Catwalking.com
123r	© Anthea Simms
124–127	Courtesy Christian Louboutin
130	Catwalking.com
131	© C. Taylor Crothers / CORBIS
132	© Nela Koenig / Retna Ltd.
133	Catwalking.com
134–135	Courtesy Roberto Cavalli
136	Photo by David Scherman / Time & Life Pictures / Getty Images
137	Catwalking.com
138	Courtesy Viktor & Rolf
139	Photo by Reg Lancaster / Express / Getty Images
140–141	Catwalking.com
142	© Anthea Simms
143	Catwalking.com
144	© RA / Lebrecht Music & Arts
145–146	Catwalking.com
147	Courtesy Roberto Cavalli
148	Catwalking.com
149l	© Anthea Simms
149r	Catwalking.com
153	The Art Archive / Centre Jeanne d'Arc, Orléans / Gianni Dagli Orti
154	Catwalking.com
155l	© Anthea Simms
155r, 156	Catwalking.com
157	© Anthea Simms
159l	Catwalking.com
159r	Everett Collection / Rex Features
160	Photo by Hulton Archive / Getty Images
161	Ronald Grant Archive
162	Rex Features
163	PARAMOUNT / THE KOBAL COLLECTION
164	Catwalking.com
165	© Anthea Simms
166–171	Catwalking.com
174	© Anthea Simms
175	Catwalking.com
176	© Anthea Simms
178	Courtesy United Nude
179	© Anthea Simms
180	Catwalking.com
181	© Anthea Simms
182	Courtesy Viktor & Rolf
183	Courtesy Stephen Venezia
184l	Courtesy Stella McCartney
184r	Catwalking.com
185	Courtesy United Nude

THANKS

This book would not have been possible without the support of the designers featured, each of whom gave generously of their time in order to provide information and images about the boots in their collections. I thank all of them for making this book such a pleasure to research and write. Along with thanking the book's commissioning and production editors, I'd like to express my appreciation to Heather Vickers, the book's picture editor, for her unwavering commitment to the project. I also thank Lovisa Burfitt for providing special illustrations for the book, which I'm certain the readers will enjoy as much as I do.

This book is dedicated to Larah Davis because she loves boots more than anyone I know. When Larah joined me on a Caribbean beach holiday she stepped off the aeroplane in a pair of boots, had three more in her suitcase and shopped for a fifth pair before heading back home. Since then, Larah's detailed descriptions of her boot-wearing antics has helped me understand why women love boots, and why men love booted women. Without these perspectives, I could not have written this book.